How to code in

Python

GCSE, iGCSE, National 4/5 and Higher

Greg Reid

HODDER
EDUCATION
AN HACHETTE UK COMPANY

Orders: please contact Hachette UK Distribution, Hely Hutchinson Centre, Milton Road, Didcot, Oxfordshire, OX11 7HH. Telephone: +44 (0)1235 827827. Email education@hachette.co.uk Lines are open from 9 a.m. to 5 p.m., Monday to Friday. You can also order through our website: www.hoddereducation.co.uk

ISBN: 978 1 5104 6182 6

© Greg Reid 2020

First published in 2020 by

Hodder Education

An Hachette UK Company,

Carmelite House, 50 Victoria Embankment

London EC4Y 0LS

Impression number   6

Year   2024

Cover photo © AndSus/stock.Adobe.com

Illustrations by Aptara Inc.

Typeset in India by Aptara Inc.

Printed and bound by CPI Group (UK) Ltd, Croydon, CR0 4YY

A catalogue record for this title is available from the British Library.

Contents

Chapter 1 – Introduction

What makes a good programmer?

Good programmers are logical thinkers. They have the ability to take a problem, break it down into its component parts and design a solution. They can then implement their solution as a sequence of instructions written in a programming language. If all this sounds like a high-level skill, well it is. Programmers are in high demand all over the world and often earn good salaries.

Although few people have this natural talent, EVERYBODY can learn to be a better programmer.

The three stages of programming

All programmers work through three stages when coding a solution to a problem.

1 The programmer must **understand the problem**. For simple problems, understanding may be almost instantaneous. More complex problems may require time, research and questioning in order to fully understand what is required.

2 The problem is broken down into smaller and smaller sub-problems in a process called **decomposition**. Depending on the complexity and size of the problem, decomposition may involve creating a formal design or it may simply take place inside the programmer's head. The purpose of decomposition is to identify the individual components (or building blocks) of the problem and programming structures that will be required to build the solution.

3 Each component is coded, tested and combined with others until a completed program solution is achieved.

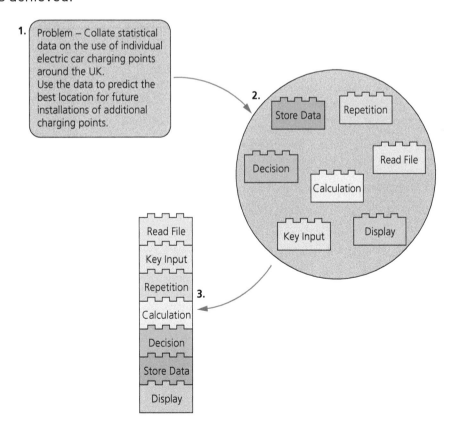

Figure 1.1: The three stages of programming

How do you become a good programmer?

Learning to program involves practising and developing several skills simultaneously:

- **Statements** (used to make **instructions**) are the building blocks of code and the tools you will require to successfully write working programs. Each section of this book begins by explaining a few new statements. The first time these are used, they will appear in **bold**. The more statements you learn and understand, the more complex the programs you can code.

- Good programmers can predict the effect of code even before they type out the actual instructions. The puzzles in each section of this book offer you the opportunity to practise this skill. Each puzzle presents you with some code and ask you to successfully predict what it will do.

- At the end of each section you will find a selection of programming problems. To code each problem, you need to identify which instructions are required to program a solution.

Finally, programming is like any other skill in that lots of practice and time will have a marked effect on your ability to code solutions to problems.

Installing Python

This book has been written for Version 3 of the Python programming language. If you are in school, college or university then you will probably already have access to the software required to code and execute (run) Python programs.

If you have purchased this book to teach yourself or to use at home, then you will need to download and install a copy of the Python 3 programming language. Python is "**open source**" software meaning that it is created, maintained and improved by an online community rather than a company. As such, it can be freely downloaded and installed from numerous websites. The official Python website is https://www.python.org.

Many Python users also download an **editor application** to write and test their Python programs. An editor will help your coding as it can provide facilities such as syntax checking (highlighting coding mistakes as you type). One editor you could use is called PyScripter but many others are freely available.

For users of tablets and smart phones there are a number of free Python Apps. These are perfect for learning the basics of Python programming and would be suitable for most of the problems and puzzles in this book. Make sure that the app you select allows you to save programs and return to them later.

Saving files

At several points throughout this book you will be challenged to solve problems by writing Python programs. As you complete each program, make sure you save your code in an organised, clearly labelled way. Some of the later problems in the book require that you continue code that you wrote to solve an earlier problem. It is a good idea to create a new folder for your all programs and give the files meaningful names, problem1 – Three In, Three Out and so on.

If an earlier program has not been saved, you may use one of the downloaded solutions as your starting point (see below).

Python code download

All the Python code in this book can be downloaded from:

www.hoddereducation.co.uk/pythonextras

The download of over 300 Python files includes:

- all the example code from each section
- every computational thinking puzzle
- solutions to every computational thinking puzzle (with explanations)
- solutions to every programming challenge (with comments)
- .txt and .csv files required to complete some of the later tasks in the book.

Try to solve the programming challenges before looking at a solution. You will be a much better programmer if you persevere and solve problems on your own.

Happy Coding!

About the author

Greg Reid started teaching Computing Science (and therefore programming) in Scottish Secondary Schools in 1994. Five years later he was promoted to head of department, a role in which he developed his love of writing teaching resources, which he has shared all over the world. Greg left teaching in 2017 to work full time for the Scottish Qualifications Authority. He is currently:

- involved with the development of Scottish school qualifications in Computing Science
- advising computing teachers across Scotland
- creating and presenting professional development opportunities for computing teachers in Scotland
- still finding the time to write the occasional teaching resource.

Section 1 – Input, output and simple calculations

Almost all computer programs are written to **input, process and output** data. For example:

- A calculator takes numbers and instructions from a keypad (input), performs the calculation requested (process) and displays the answer on the calculator's small screen (output).

- A washing machine senses the weight of clothes (input) and the selected wash cycle from the machine's control panel (input). The amount of water required and length of the wash cycle are calculated (process). Electrical signals are sent to pumps, heaters and motors to control the wash cycle (output).

While it would be great to write program code that reads data from sensors or controls a water pump, the first steps in learning to program usually involve writing simple code that

- allows the user to enter text or numbers using the keyboard (input)
- changes the text or performs simple mathematical calculations with numbers (process)
- displays text or numbers on the user's screen (output).

In programming, the user is the person who will use the executing (running) program.

Chapter 2 – Examples of input, output and simple calculations

Some examples of Python 3 input and output instructions are shown below. Try typing each of these programs into your Python editor. **Execute** (run) the code and observe what happens.

Example 1 – Output using a simple print( ) statement

To display text or numbers on the user's screen we use the **print( )** statement.

Notice that displaying text requires quotation marks " " around the words, while displaying numbers does not.

▼ Program Code

```
print("Hello World")
print("I am")
print(44)
print("years old.")
```

Output (as seen on the user's screen)   ☒

```
Hello World
I am
44
years old.
```

Each print( ) statement will display its output on a new line.

Example 2 – Output using a complex print( ) statement

A print( ) statement can be made up of several parts, with each part separated by a comma.

Note that Python automatically replaces the comma with a space when the output is displayed.

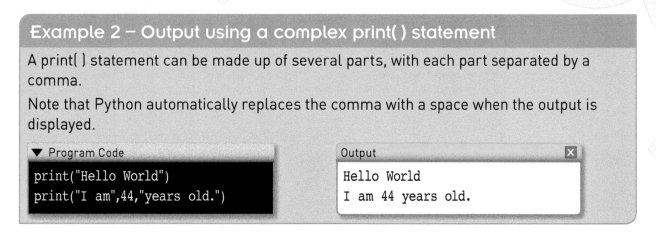

▼ Program Code

```
print("Hello World")
print("I am",44,"years old.")
```

Output   ☒

```
Hello World
I am 44 years old.
```

Example 3 – Keyboard input using a simple input( ) statement

Input statements are used to ask the user to type in text or numbers.

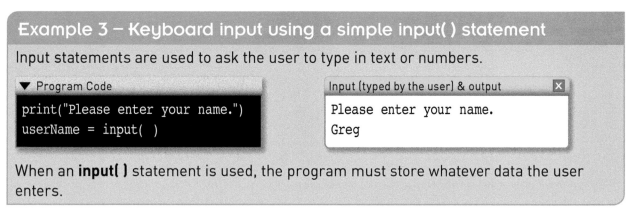

▼ Program Code

```
print("Please enter your name.")
userName = input( )
```

Input (typed by the user) & output   ☒

```
Please enter your name.
Greg
```

When an **input( )** statement is used, the program must store whatever data the user enters.

Variables

The second line of the code in Example 3 above creates a **variable** (or storage location) called "userName". When the user types the name (enters text) and then presses enter, the keyboard input "Greg" is stored in the variable.

You might want to imagine variables as boxes that your program temporarily stores data in while it's running.

A variable can be given almost any name made up of letters and numbers. Some exceptions to this are:

- You cannot use two or more separate words as a variable name. Note that this book uses camel case (using capital letters in the middle of a word) in place of two words. For example, "userName" instead of "user name".

- In Python, variable names should always start with a lower case letter. This is because capital letters are reserved for something else.

- A variable cannot be called any of the statement words of the Python language. For example, "print" or "input" would not be valid variable names.

Example 4 – Keyboard input, with a message to the user

An input( ) statement may include a suitable message inside quotation marks " ".

▼ Program Code

```
userName = input("Please enter your name.")
print("Hello",userName)
```

Input (typed by the user) & output ☒

```
Please enter your name. Greg
Hello Greg
```

The print( ) statement is used this time to display some text and the variable "userName". Note that when you print a variable, you display what the variable is currently storing. In this example that will be whatever the user typed in.

Example 5 – Inputting the correct data type

Simple programs will input and store three different types of data:
- **Strings** – text
- **Integers** – whole numbers with no decimal places
- Real numbers – numbers with decimal places (sometimes called floating point numbers or floats).

In programming, string, integer and float (or real) are called **data types**.

▼ Program Code

```
location = str(input("Where are you?"))
hour = int(input("What hour is it?"))
temp = float(input("What is the temperature?"))
print("It is", temp, "degrees at", hour, "hours in", location)
```

Controlled input types and complex output ☒

```
Where are you? Paris
What hour is it? 18
What is the temperature? 22.5
It is 22.5 degrees at 18 hours in Paris
```

An input( ) statement can be contained with **str( )**, **int( )** or **float( )** statements to ensure that the correct type of data will be entered by your user. If the user enters the wrong type of data the program may display an error message and crash.

Example 6 – Concatenation

In programming, concatenation means to join two strings together.

▼ Program Code

```
firstName = str(input("What is your first name?"))
surname = str(input("What is your surname?"))
print(firstName,surname)
print(firstName+surname)
```

Controlled input types and complex output ☒

```
What is your first name? Evelyn
What is your surname? Phair
Evelyn Phair
EvelynPhair
```

The second print( ) statement uses the + symbol to concatenate the two variables "firstName" and "surname". Note the difference between the outputs produced by the two print lines. When strings are concatenated, they are literally joined together and displayed without a space.

Chapter 3 – Computational thinking puzzles (input and output)

Any good programmer is able to predict what their code will do. Learning to predict the effect of code will improve your ability to read code, write code and solve problems. This skill is known as 'computational thinking'.

The puzzles throughout this book will improve your computational thinking skills. Each puzzle consists of a short bit of code. You will be asked to predict the output produced when each short program is executed.

For example, the following code would produce the output shown below.

Program code (question)

```
street = "Dover Drive"
donation1 = 120
donation2 = 80
donation3 = 60
print("The total donations for",street,"are:",donation1, donation2, donation3)
```

Output from program (answer)

```
The total donations for Dover Drive are: 120 80 60
```

Puzzle set 1 – Input and output

For each of the following puzzles, think through the code and write down the exact output produced by the code (including any spaces). The puzzles deliberately get harder.

1
```
productName = "Bicycle Chain"
print(productName)
```
Output

2
```
dogBreed = "Labradoodle"
dogAge = "Two"
print(dogBreed, dogAge)
```
Output

3
```
name = "Scott"
age = 23
print(name, "aged", age)
```
Output

4
```
coffee = "Lava Java"
print(coffee + coffee)
```
Output

5   State the output if the user enters "video".
```
game = input("Please enter a word")
print(game, game + game)
```
Output

6
```
var1 = "Going"
var2 = "Gone"
print(var1, "Going" + var2)
```
Output

7
```
print("This,"+" is a plus +","symbol")
```
Output

8
```
textOne = "Be kind"
textTwo = "possible"
textThree = textOne + " whenever"
print(textThree, textTwo + ".")
```

Output

9
```
con1 = "c"
vowl = "e"
con2 = "m"
print("energy(" + vowl + ") =", con2 + con1, "squared")
```

Output

10 For this puzzle, state the two inputs that would produce the output shown below.

Output

Love the life you live. Live the life you love.

```
word1 = input("Please enter the first word")
word2 = "the " + word1 + " you"
word3 = input("Please enter the first word")
print("Love", word2, word3 + ". Live the", word1, "you love.")
```

Input

Chapter 4 – Examples of simple calculations

Simple calculations in programs either involve using values entered directly into the code or values stored in variables. The results of a calculation may be displayed immediately or stored in a variable for use later.

Python, like most programming languages, uses slightly different mathematical symbols for multiplication and division.

- **multiplication** is represented by an **asterix (*)**.
- **division** is represented by a forward **slash (/)**.

Some examples of simple Python 3 calculations are shown below. Type each of these programs into your Python editor and execute them to see what happens.

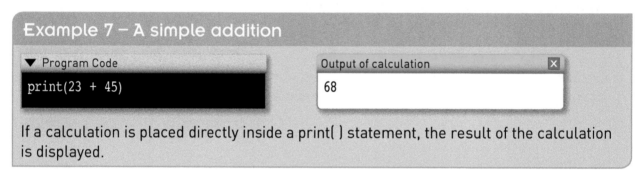

Example 7 – A simple addition

Program Code
```
print(23 + 45)
```

Output of calculation
```
68
```

If a calculation is placed directly inside a print( ) statement, the result of the calculation is displayed.

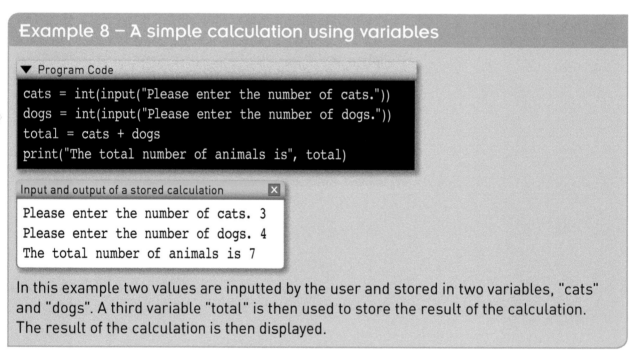

Example 8 – A simple calculation using variables

Program Code
```
cats = int(input("Please enter the number of cats."))
dogs = int(input("Please enter the number of dogs."))
total = cats + dogs
print("The total number of animals is", total)
```

Input and output of a stored calculation
```
Please enter the number of cats. 3
Please enter the number of dogs. 4
The total number of animals is 7
```

In this example two values are inputted by the user and stored in two variables, "cats" and "dogs". A third variable "total" is then used to store the result of the calculation. The result of the calculation is then displayed.

Example 9 – Basic maths rules apply in programming too

Basic mathematical rules also apply to programming.

- Calculations within brackets should be performed first.
- Division (/) and multiplication (*) are carried out before addition (+) or subtract ion (-).

Mathematical rules can cause errors in programs if not used correctly. For example, imagine a program written to calculate the average of three numbers: 3, 6 and 9. Brackets would be required to ensure the addition of the three numbers takes place before the total is divided by three:

(3+6+9)/3

If the brackets are left out, the resulting calculation is interpreted as:

3+6+ 9/3

Here, 9 is divided by 3 before the other two numbers are added on.

The correct calculation gives an average of 6. Without the brackets, the average is incorrectly calculated as 12.

▼ Program Code

```
answer = 4 + 2 * 3
answer2 = (10 + 2) / 3
print(answer)
print(answer2)
```

Output of calculations ☒

```
10
4.0
```

Example 10 – Data types, int( ) and float( )

As stated earlier, numbers may be one of two data types: integers (whole numbers) or floats (decimal numbers).

Many programming languages are very rigid regarding the use of data types. In these languages, if you declare a variable as storing an integer, it can only ever store integers.

Python is not as rigid as this and will change from storing integer to float (or float to integer) depending on a few simple rules.

- If a calculation involves division then the answer is always stored as a float.
  10/2 = 5.0 (not 5).
- If a calculation involves a mixture of integer and float numbers, the result is always stored as a float.
- If the built-in function int( ) is used, the number involved is forcibly stored as an integer. The decimal places are removed by the int( ) function:
  int(75.8) = 75
- If the function float( ) is used, the number is forcibly stored as a decimal number:
  float(45) = 45.0

▼ Program Code

```
number = 5 + 2.5
print(number)
number2 = number/3
print(number2)
number3 = int(number2) * 4
print(number3)
```

Output of calculations ☒

```
7.5
2.5
8
```

Chapter 5 – Computational thinking puzzles (simple calculations)

The text and/or numbers stored in a variable are updated when they are assigned a new value.

Program code

```
num1 = 5
num1 = 7+2
print(num1)
```

```
Output
9
```

The output is 9 because the original value 5, stored in the variable num1, is replaced by the result of 7+2 in the second line of code.

This is an important concept in programming as many programs involve constantly storing, updating and outputting text or numbers. This also highlights a potential problem when writing programs: errors can be created by accidentally replacing text and numbers you wish to keep.

Puzzle set 2 – Simple calculations

For each of the following puzzles, think through the code and write down the exact output produced. Pay attention to:

- **whether the answer should be written as an integer or float number**
- **when the numbers stored in variables are updated.**

As before, the puzzles will get harder.

11 `print(12/6)`

```
Output

```

12 `print(13+7–2)`

```
Output

```

13 `print(4*4)`

```
Output

```

14 `print(int(6/2) + 3)`

```
Output

```

15 `print((7+3)/2)`

```
Output

```

16 `print((12+6+2)/(3+2))`

```
Output

```

17
```
numberOne = 6
numberTwo = 13
print(numberOne + numberTwo)
```

Output

18
```
numberOne = 5
numberTwo = 16
numberThree = numberOne * numberTwo
print(numberThree)
```

Output

Output

19
```
numberOne = 5
numberTwo = numberOne * 2
numberThree = numberOne + numberTwo + numberTwo
print(numberOne,numberTwo,numberThree)
```

20
```
numberOne = 20 / 4
numberTwo = numberOne + 55
numberThree = numberTwo / 6
print(numberOne,numberTwo,numberThree)
```

Output

21 State the output if the user enters 7.
```
numberOne = int(input("Please enter an integer."))
numberTwo = numberOne * numberOne
numberThree = numberTwo / numberOne
print(int(numberThree * numberThree))
```

Output

22
```
numberOne = 12 + 8
numberThree = numberOne * 3
numberTwo = numberThree - 55
numberThree = numberTwo * (numberOne / 2)
numberOne = numberThree + 17
print(numberOne)
```

Output

23
```
numberOne = int(12 / 4)
numberTwo = 6 * 2
numberThree = 4 + 1
numberThree = numberTwo
numberTwo = float(numberOne)
numberThree = numberOne
print(numberOne, numberTwo, numberThree)
```

Output

Chapter 6 – Examples of simple string functions

One of the great things about Python is the sheer number of built-in **functions** contained within the programming language. Built-in functions are small pieces of pre-written code that provide additional features for a programmer to use, without having to code the features themselves.

Let's look at a few built-in functions that can be used in Python to manipulate strings (text).

Example 11 – Using substring to extract part of a string

Substring is when code is used to extract some of the text characters from a string. In Python, this is achieved using square brackets containing two values (the start and end point of the substring selection) separated by a colon. For example:

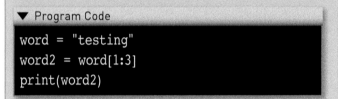

```
word = "testing"
word2 = word[1:3]
print(word2)
```

Output
```
es
```

The numbers in the square brackets refer to a point between each character in the string. These can be positive numbers (counting each point from left to right) or negative numbers (counting from right to left) as shown in the example below.

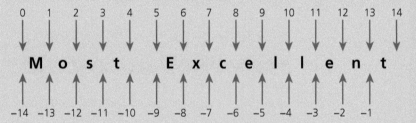

Figure 6.1: Substring counting

If either value is missed out the substring defaults to the first or last character.

```
comment = "Most Excellent"
part1 = comment[0:7]
print(part1)
print(comment[-5:-2])
print(comment[:3])
print(comment[-9:])
```

Output
```
Most Ex
lle
Mos
Excellent
```

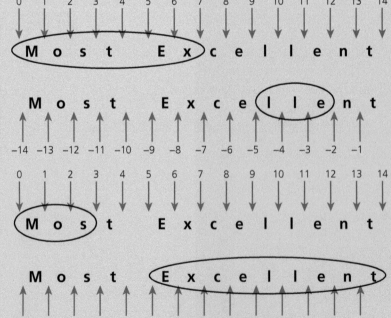

Example 12 – Changing the case of text

The **lower( )** and **upper( )** functions convert strings to lower or upper case characters. Note that lower( ) and upper() are used by typing a full stop after the variable name followed by the function.

▼ Program Code

```
quotation = "The answer is Forty Two"
smallQuotation = quotation.lower()
print(smallQuotation)
print(quotation.upper())
```

Output ☒

```
the answer is forty two
THE ANSWER IS FORTY TWO
```

Example 13 – Calculating the Number of Characters in a String

The length function, **len( )**, counts the number of characters (including spaces) in a string.

▼ Program Code

```
sentence = "I never could get the hang of Thursdays"
print("There are", len(sentence),"characters in the sentence.")
```

Output ☒

```
There are 39 characters in the sentence.
```

Example 14 – Counting the occurrence of one string in another

The **count( )** function returns the number of times one string appears in another string.

The count function is case sensitive so in the example below only two occurrences of "s" are found. The capital S is not counted.

▼ Program Code

```
sentence = "Six rain ridden summers"
print(sentence.count("s"))
```

Output ☒

```
2
```

Example 15 – Replacing text within a string

The **replace( )** function searches for some given text within a string and replaces it with alternative text.

▼ Program Code

```
motto = "Work Hard, Study Hard"
newMotto = motto.replace("Hard","Well")
print(newMotto)
```

Output ☒

```
Work Well, Study Well
```

The above code replaces the text "Hard" with the text "Well". The rest of the string remains unchanged.

Chapter 7 – Computational thinking puzzles (string functions)

This set of puzzles are all about manipulating strings using functions. Read each piece of code carefully, paying particular attention to where functions have been used. The puzzles start as very simple problems and end with some fairly tricky ones.

Write down the output produced by the code in each of the following puzzles.

Puzzle set 3 – String functions

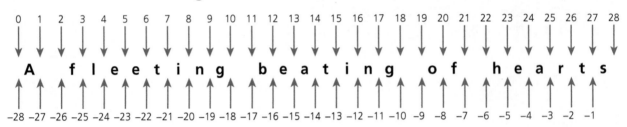

24
```
lyric = "A fleeting beating of hearts"
print(lyric[0:6])
```
Output

25
```
lyric = "A fleeting beating of hearts"
print(lyric[:14])
```
Output

26
```
lyric = "A fleeting beating of hearts"
print(lyric[20:])
```
Output

27
```
lyric = "A fleeting beating of hearts"
print(lyric[-4:])
```
Output

28
```
lyric = "A fleeting beating of hearts"
print(lyric[5:-15])
```
Output

29
```
lyric = "A fleeting beating of hearts"
lyric2 = lyric[2:10]
print(lyric2[4:])
```
Output

30
```
firstName = "Gillian"
surname = "Coltart"
print(firstName[0:1] + surname[:1])
```

Output

31
```
filmRelease = "Car Wars Return of the Mini"
tempFilm = filmRelease.lower()
print(tempFilm)
```

Output

32
```
filmRelease = "World War Z"
releaseDate = "31st OCT"
tempFilm = filmRelease.upper()
tempDate = releaseDate.lower()
print(tempFilm + " " + tempDate)
```

Output

33
```
word1 = "central"
word2 = "processing"
word3 = "unit"
word4 = word1[0:1].upper()
word5 = word2[0:1].upper()
word6 = word3[0:1].upper()
print(word4 + " = " + word1)
print(word5 + " = " + word2)
print(word6 + " = " + word3)
```

Output

34
```
password = "beetle man"
passwordLength = len(password)
print(passwordLength)
```

Output

35
```
password = "Sphinx"
passwordLength = len(password)
print("Your password", password, "is", passwordLength, "characters long")
```

Output

36
```
quotation = "There are only two kinds
   of people who are really fascinating:
   people who know absolutely everything,
   and people who know absolutely nothing. - Oscar Wilde"
print(quotation.count("re"))
```

Output

37
```
quotation = "Whatever you are, be a bad one. Abraham Lincoln"
quotationNew = quotation.replace ("bad","good")
print(quotationNew)
```

Output

38
```
quotation = "I met an old lady once,
   almost a hundred years old, and she
   told me…"
quotation = quotation.replace("lady","gentleman")
quotation = quotation.replace("she","he")
print(quotation)
```

Output

39
```
word = "Code & Coding"
word = word.replace("Code","Programs")
print(word)
print(len(word))
```

Output

40
```
password = "02jjkk kkde"
password = password.replace("kk","ddd")
password = password.replace("jj","j")
print("Number of characters in password =",len(password))
```

Output

41
```
sentenceOne = "The to boys learned to new skills"
sentenceTwo = sentenceOne.replace("to","two")
sentenceThree = sentenceTwo.replace("boys","girls")
totalLetterW = sentenceOne.count("w")+sentenceTwo.count("w")+sentenceThree.count("w")
totalLetterB = sentenceOne.count("b")+sentenceTwo.count("b")+sentenceThree.count("b")
print(totalLetterW+totalLetterB)
```

Output

42 The following program uses string handling to create and display a simple password.

Work out what the password is.

```
statement = "When Mr. Bilbo Baggins of Bag End announced"
letter1position = statement.count("a")
letter2position = statement.count("e")
letter3position = statement.count("i")
letter4position = statement.count("o")
letter1 = statement[letter1position-1:letter1position]
letter2 = statement[letter2position-1:letter2position+2]
letter3 = statement[letter3position-1:letter3position]
letter4 = statement[letter4position+1:letter4position+3]
password = letter2 + letter4 + letter3 + letter1
print(password)
```

Output

Chapter 8 – Examples of simple mathematical functions

Python also includes many built-in functions used to manipulate numbers. A few examples of mathematical functions are shown below.

Example 16 – Rounding decimal numbers

The **round( )** function reduces the number of decimal places in a number rounding up or down as required.

The round( ) function should contain two values in the brackets, separated by a comma:

- The first is the number to be rounded. This may be a number or a variable storing a number.
- The second is the number of decimal places the number is to be rounded to.

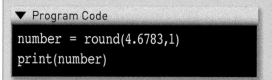

▼ Program Code
```
number = round(4.6783,1)
print(number)
```

Output
```
4.7
```

The correct computing term for these values is parameters. We say that parameters are passed into the function. The function then returns the result: in this case a rounded number.

Example 17 – Truncating a decimal number

We've seen the integer function already. The **int( )** function truncates (shortens) a decimal number (float), rounding it down to the nearest integer by removing all the decimal places.

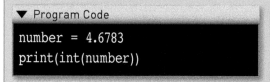

▼ Program Code
```
number = 4.6783
print(int(number))
```

Output
```
4
```

Example 18 – Always rounding up

The ceiling function **math.ceil( )**, rounds a real number up to the nearest integer.

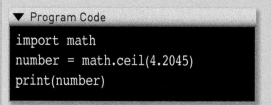

▼ Program Code
```
import math
number = math.ceil(4.2045)
print(number)
```

Output
```
5
```

The first word of this function, "math", is a module library (collection) of extra mathematical functions that can be added to Python to extend the capabilities of the programming language.

This function requires "import math" at the top of your program. This line adds lots of additional maths functions to the standard capabilities of Python.

Example 19 – Modulus, calculating the remainder

The **modulus** function **%** calculates the remainder when one number is divided by another.

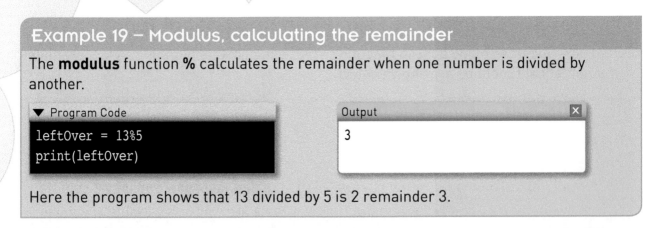

▼ Program Code

```
leftOver = 13%5
print(leftOver)
```

Output

```
3
```

Here the program shows that 13 divided by 5 is 2 remainder 3.

Example 20 – To the power of

The **pow( )** function multiplies one number to the power of another number. The example shows 4^2.

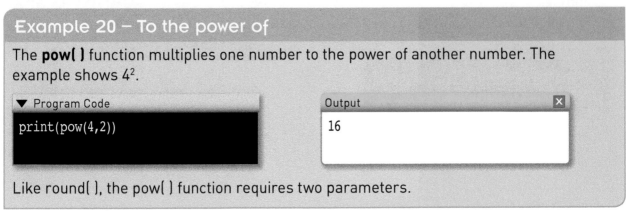

▼ Program Code

```
print(pow(4,2))
```

Output

```
16
```

Like round( ), the pow( ) function requires two parameters.

Chapter 9 – Computational thinking puzzles (mathematical functions)

Never underestimate the value of maths when programming. The majority of programs require some form of calculation to be carried out. If your aim is to be a games programmer or something similar, then your maths will have to be very good!

Puzzle set 4 – Mathematical functions

43
```
height = 193.734
print(round(height,2))
```
Output

44
```
shoeSize = 10.3
print(round(shoeSize,0))
```
Output

45
```
import math
weight = 78.65
print(math.ceil(weight))
```
Output

46
```
offcut = 25%7
print(offcut)
```
Output

47
```
import math
value = 12.5%3
print(math.ceil(value))
```
Output

48
```
import math
roomLength = 20
plank = 3
woodNeeded = math.ceil(roomLength/plank)
print("The number of whole planks needed =",woodNeeded)
```
Output

49
```
import math
value = 57.884
decimal = value − int(value)
print(round(decimal,2))
```
Output

50
```
cat = 5.91
dog = int(cat)
print(pow(dog,2))
```
Output

51
```
import math
num1 = 12.7
num2 = 30.3
num3 = (int(num2) - math.ceil(num1))
num4 = pow(3,(num3%5))
print(num4*(int(num2/10)))
```
Output

Chapter 10 – Programming challenges for Section 1

Below is a collection of programming challenges. For each challenge you are required to write Python code to solve the problem. Each of the problems involves using the Python statements, syntax and functions that you have learned in Section 1.

Statements and Syntax	Text Functions
• input( )	• str( )
• print( )	• int( )
• " "	• float( )
• ,	• .lower( )
• +	• .upper( )
• -	• len( )
• /	• .count( )
• *	• .replace( )
• ( )	**Maths Functions**
• %	• round( )
• [:]	• math.ceil( )
• variableName =	• pow( )

Although the above already looks like a long list, you have only scratched the surface of Python. No professional programmer memorises every statement and function they use. If you are not sure of how to write a particular statement, you can always refer back to examples.

Program Challenges for input and output

Program 1 – Three in, three out

Write a program that will allow a user to enter their name (string), their age (integer) and their favourite TV programme (string). The program will then display the information entered and some additional text on separate lines.

An example of the input and output from the program is shown below.

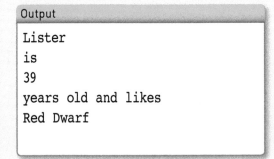

```
Input
Please enter your name.
Lister
What is your age?
39
What is your favourite TV programme?
Red Dwarf
```

```
Output
Lister
is
39
years old and likes
Red Dwarf
```

Program 2 – Name swapper

Write a program that requires the user to type in their first name and surname. The program will then display the two names in reverse order.

```
Input
David
Tennant
```

```
Output
Tennant David
```

Program 3 – Three in, three out (formatted)

Open and edit program 1 so that the information entered is displayed differently as shown in the output box below. Note – your output will now have to display variables and text together.

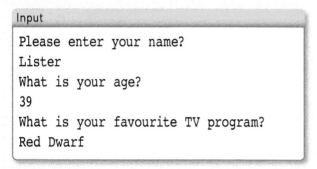
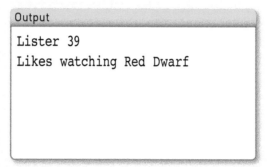

```
Input
Please enter your name?
Lister
What is your age?
39
What is your favourite TV program?
Red Dwarf
```

```
Output
Lister 39
Likes watching Red Dwarf
```

Program 4 – Postcode formatter

Your user is required to enter the four separate sections of a UK postcode, which takes the form:

   letters, number, number, letters

Once entered, the postcode should be displayed with a space in the middle.

```
Input
KY
8
9
HL
```

```
Output
KY8 9HL
```

Program 5 – Calculate the area of a rectangle

Ask your user to enter the length and width of a rectangle. Your program should calculate the area of the rectangle (length×width) and display the result with a suitable message.

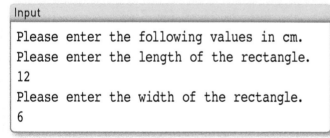
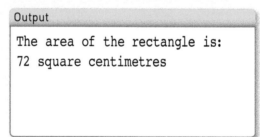

```
Input
Please enter the following values in cm.
Please enter the length of the rectangle.
12
Please enter the width of the rectangle.
6
```

```
Output
The area of the rectangle is:
72 square centimetres
```

Program 6 – Number generator

Write a program that inputs two individual integers between 0 and 9. The program should then perform a calculation and store a single number in a third variable called "total". The total should then be displayed on the screen.

```
Input
2
6
```

```
Output
26
```

The following challenges all use substring and the string functions (lower, upper, len, count and replace) explained in Examples 11–15 and covered by Puzzles 24–42.

Program 7 – Postcode formatter (part 2)

Edit program 4 to ensure that the postcode is always displayed in upper case letters, even if the user inputs the letters in lower case.

```
Input
KY
8
9
hl
```

```
Output
KY8 9HL
```

Program 8 – Name length

Write a program that asks the user to enter their forename and surname. The program should output the total numbers of letters in their name.

```
Input
Please enter your forename:
David
Please enter your surname:
Stott
```

```
Output
There are 10 letters in your name.
```

Program 9 – Counting vowels

Write a program that asks the user to enter a sentence of their choice. The program should then calculate and display the number of times each vowel appears in the sentence along with the total number of vowels. Make sure the program counts both upper case and lower case vowels.

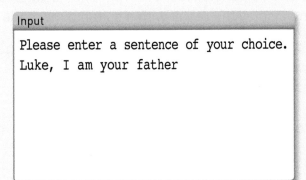
```
Input
Please enter a sentence of your choice.
Luke, I am your father
```

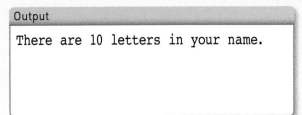
```
Output
Your sentence contained the following:
a = 2
e = 2
i = 1
o = 1
u = 2
This is a total of 8 vowels.
```

Program 10 – Changing gender

A program is required to change a male student's school report comment into a similar comment for a female student. The program should change any example of his to her and he to she.

Input

```
Please enter the male report.
He should always ensure that his answers contain as much detail as possible.
```

Output

```
The female comment is:
She should always ensure that her answers contain as much detail as possible.
```

Program 11 – Stock code generator

A program is required to generate stock codes for a supermarket. Ask the user to enter the name of a new product along with the year. The program should combine the first and last two letters of the product to the first and last characters of the year to create the code.

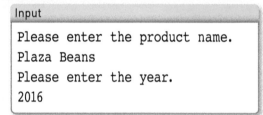

Input

```
Please enter the product name.
Plaza Beans
Please enter the year.
2016
```

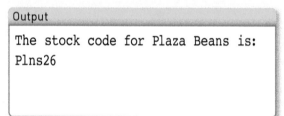

Output

```
The stock code for Plaza Beans is:
Plns26
```

The following challenges all use the mathematical functions (round, int, ceil, % and pow) explained in Examples 16–20 and covered by Puzzles 43–51.

Program 12 – Auction fee

A program is required to calculate the fee charged by an auction company when goods are sold. The program should add up the costs of three items sold and calculate the fee, which is 10% of the total cost. Fees are rounded to the nearest whole number.

Input

```
Please enter your three costs.
12.78
6.32
34.99
```

Output

```
The total cost is £54.09
The auction companies
fee is £5.0.
```

Program 13 – Calculate the area of a circle

Ask your user to enter the radius of a circle. Your program should use what they have entered to calculate the area of the circle and display the result.

Area
=
$3.14 \times r^2$

Input
```
Please enter the following value in cm.
Please enter the radius of the circle.
16
```

Output
```
The area of the circle is:
803.84 square centimetres
```

Program 14 – Prize draw cheat

You think you can win your football club's "how many sweets are in the jar?" prize draw. Assuming that you have already calculated the volumes of one sweet and the jar, write a program to input these two volumes and output the number of whole sweets that fit in the jar.

Input
```
Please enter the volume of the jar (cm3):
2712.96
Please enter the volume of one sweet (cm3):
2.12
```

Output
```
1279 sweets fit into the jar.
```

Program 15 – Leftover paint

A painter requires a simple program that will calculate and display the number of pots of paint required to complete a job. The program should also display the area (in metres squared) that could be painted with the leftover paint.

Input
```
Enter the area in m2 to be painted.
178
Enter the area (m2) that a single pot covers.
25
```

Output
```
You will need 8 pots of paint.
You can paint 3.0 m2 with the leftover paint.
```

Often the complexity of a program is increased by the complexity of the problem scenario. A good programmer must be able to examine and understand scenarios they may have never encountered previously. The last few program challenges have more complex scenarios. Read each one carefully to understand what is required.

Program 16 – Laying bricks

A bricklayer needs to calculate if they have part of a brick left over when they build a wall of a certain length. Write a program that asks for the length of a brick in centimetres along with the length of the wall in metres. The program should add 1 cm to the length of each brick (to allow for concrete between the bricks) and then calculate the number of bricks required to build one row of the wall. The program should also display any centimetres left over once a single row of bricks of one row is laid.

Input
```
Please enter the length of a brick in cm:
20
Please enter the length of the wall in m:
9.89
```

Output
```
47 bricks build one row of wall.
This is 2 cm short of the required wall length.
```

Program 17 – Calculating the atomic weight of hydrocarbons (alkanes)

A hydrocarbon is a molecule made up of linked carbon (C) atoms with hydrogen (H) atoms branching off each carbon. Your program will ask the user to enter the number of carbon atoms in a hydrocarbon and use the number entered to then calculate the number of hydrogen atoms using the formula below. Both numbers should be stored.

```
number of H atoms = (number of C atoms × 2) + 2
```

The atomic weight of the molecule is then calculated by multiplying the number of carbon atoms by 12 and adding the number of hydrogen atoms. The number of C and H atoms along with the atomic weight should be displayed as shown in the output below.

Input
```
Enter the number of carbon atoms.
3
```

Output
```
The atomic mass of C3H8 is 44
```

Program 18 – Standard scratch

The "standard scratch score" of a golf course is calculated by adding together the number of shots it should take to complete each hole. This score is then adjusted depending on the difficulty of the course.

Hole	1	2	3	4	5	6	7	8	9	OUT
Adam	5	6	6	5	5	4	6	5	4	46
Sheida	4	3	5	4	5	4	5	4	4	38
Par	3	5	3	3	4	3	4	3	3	31

For example:

2 holes should take 5 shots (par 5)

$2 \times 5 = 10$

10 holes should take 4 shots (par 4)

$10 \times 4 = 40$

6 holes should take 3 shots (par 3)

$6 \times 3 = 18$

$10 + 40 + 18 = 68$ shots in total

Difficulty adjustment = -2 68 shots $- 2 = 66$

Standard Scratch = 66

Input
```
How many par 3 holes are there?
6
How many par 4 holes are there?
10
How many par 5 holes are there?
2
What is the difficulty adjustment for the course?
-2
```

Output
```
The Standard Scratch score for the course is:
66
```

Program 19 – Cycling speed

Many cyclists use a bicycle computer to display their speed and distance. The computer measures the number of times the bike's front wheel has rotated and multiples this by circumference of the front tyre to calculate the distance travelled. If the computer also knows how long the cyclist has been travelling for, the average speed can also be calculated.

Write a program to simulate a bicycle computer. The user should input the circumference of the wheel in millimetres, the number of wheel revolutions and the number of minutes the cyclist has been travelling. The program should calculate the kilometres travelled and the average speed in km per hour.

speed (kmph) = distance (kilometres) / time (hours)

```
Input

What is the circumference of your wheel in millimetres?
1250
How many wheel revolutions have taken place in your journey?
8920
How many minutes did you cycle for?
30
```

```
Output

You covered 11.15 km.
At an average speed of 22.3 kmh.
```

Section 2 – Selection (if) statements

Programs may have to respond differently to a variety of inputs and calculations. The ability to make decisions and then select which part of a program will execute is a vital part of programming.

The flow chart below shows a simple program design.

We can see from the design that, depending on the total price, the program must perform only one of two different calculations.

A **selection statement** examines a condition and then makes a decision based on the result. If the condition is found to be true then the program will execute one or more lines of code.

Blocks of code

Selection statements are written as blocks of code. Programming languages use a variety of ways to show whether code is part of statement. Python uses:

- a colon (:)
- followed by indented code.

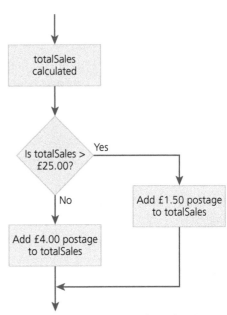

Fig 11.1: Flowchart showing simple program design

To indent code means to move it to the right compared to the line above, as shown with the two print statements below.

```
ticket = str(input("Enter another ticket: child/adult/concession"))
if ticket == "child":
    print("Remember there are height restrictions on some rides")
    print("Please read all signs carefully before queuing")
ticket = str(input("Enter another ticket: child/adult/concession"))
```

The block of code ends when the next line of the program isn't indented. Thus the final line above is not part of the selection statement.

Beware! Incorrect indentation can cause errors in your code. If the second print statement were not indented, it would be outside the selection block. If it were outside, this would change how it displays its message – it would always display its message and not just when ticket == "child".

Chapter 11 – Examples of selection (if) statements

Some examples of Python "if" statements with conditions code are shown below. Try typing each of these programs into your Python editor and run them to see what happens.

Example 21 – A simple "if" statement

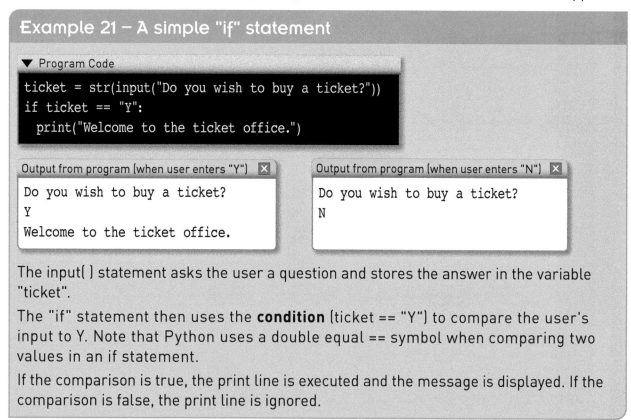

▼ Program Code

```
ticket = str(input("Do you wish to buy a ticket?"))
if ticket == "Y":
    print("Welcome to the ticket office.")
```

Output from program (when user enters "Y") ☒
```
Do you wish to buy a ticket?
Y
Welcome to the ticket office.
```

Output from program (when user enters "N") ☒
```
Do you wish to buy a ticket?
N
```

The input( ) statement asks the user a question and stores the answer in the variable "ticket".

The "if" statement then uses the **condition** (ticket == "Y") to compare the user's input to Y. Note that Python uses a double equal == symbol when comparing two values in an if statement.

If the comparison is true, the print line is executed and the message is displayed. If the comparison is false, the print line is ignored.

Example 22 – An "else" statement

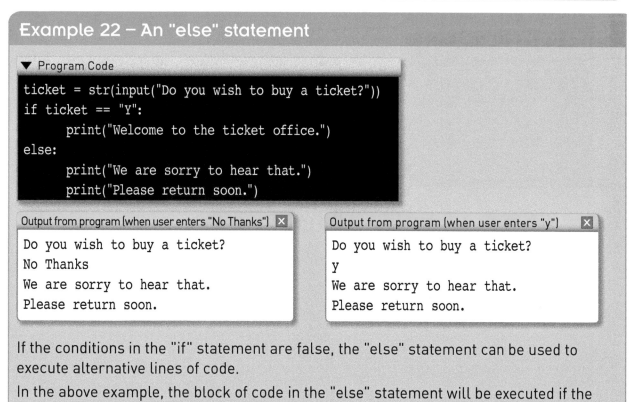

▼ Program Code

```
ticket = str(input("Do you wish to buy a ticket?"))
if ticket == "Y":
        print("Welcome to the ticket office.")
else:
        print("We are sorry to hear that.")
        print("Please return soon.")
```

Output from program (when user enters "No Thanks") ☒
```
Do you wish to buy a ticket?
No Thanks
We are sorry to hear that.
Please return soon.
```

Output from program (when user enters "y") ☒
```
Do you wish to buy a ticket?
y
We are sorry to hear that.
Please return soon.
```

If the conditions in the "if" statement are false, the "else" statement can be used to execute alternative lines of code.

In the above example, the block of code in the "else" statement will be executed if the user enters anything other than "Y" (the result of the condition would be false). Because the comparison is case sensitive, a small "y" would also be false.

Example 23 – An "if" statement with mathematical operators

▼ Program Code

```
year = int(input("Please enter a year."))
if year < 1969:
    print("No moon landings yet.")
if year >= 1969:
    print("Man has walked on the moon!")
```

Output from program (when user enters "1953") ⊠

```
Please enter a year.
1953
No moon landings yet.
```

Output from program (when user enters "1992") ⊠

```
Please enter a year.
1992
Man has walked on the moon!
```

When numbers are used in comparisons, the following symbols, called operators, may be used in the conditions:

> greater than   >= greater than or equal to   != not equal to

< less than   <= less than or equal to

Example 24 – Complex conditions (and, or)

▼ Program Code

```
ticket = str(input("Do you wish to buy a ticket?"))
if ticket == "Y":
    print("Welcome to the ticket office.")
else:
    print("We are sorry to hear that.")
    print("Please return soon.")
age = int(input("Please enter your age"))
if age >= 5 and age <= 17:
    print("Please purchase a junior ticket")
if age > 17 and age < 65:
    print("Please purchase an adult ticket")
if age >= 65:
    print("You are entitled to a senior ticket")
```

Output from program (when user enters "Y") ⊠

```
Do you wish to buy a ticket?
Y
Welcome to the ticket office.
Please enter your age
23
Please purchase an adult ticket
```

Output from program (when user enters "N") ⊠

```
Do you wish to buy a ticket?
N
Please enter your age
15
Please purchase an junior ticket
```

A complex condition is built from two or more comparisons.

The comparisons are combined as follows:

and   both conditions must be true   age > 17 and age < 65

or   only one of the conditions must be true   age < 17 or age >= 65

Did you spot the logic error in Example 24?

If the user does not wish to buy a ticket "N", they are still asked their age. The program should only ask the user their age after they have decided to buy a ticket.

To change this in the program, the highlighted code would have to be moved from the bottom of the program to inside the first "if" statement, as shown below. Note that the code now has two levels of indentation.

▼ Program Code

```
ticket = str(input("Do you wish to buy a ticket?"))
if ticket == "Y":
    print("Welcome to the ticket office.")
    age = int(input("Please enter your age"))
    if age >= 5 and age <= 17:
        print("Please purchase a junior ticket")
    if age > 17 and age < 65:
        print("Please purchase an adult ticket")
    if age >= 65:
        print("You are entitled to a senior ticket")
else:
    print("We are sorry to hear that.")
    print("Please return soon.")
```

The highlighted code is now only executed when the user enters "Y" at the beginning of the program. One "if" statement inside another like this is said to be **nested**.

When programming, the order and position of code can be as important as the actual lines of code you write.

Example 25 – Else if (elif)

In the following code, "elif" is used instead of multiple "if" statements.

The advantage of this format is that as soon as one of the comparisons is true, none of the remaining code in the block is executed. This is more efficient than separate "if" statements where each "if" statement would be executed even after one comparison is found to be true.

▼ Program Code

```python
age = int(input("Please enter your age"))
if age >= 0 and age < 5:
    print("Sorry, You are too young to attend")
elif age >= 5 and age < 18:
    print("Please purchase a junior ticket")
elif age >= 18 and age < 65:
    print("Please purchase an adult ticket")
elif age >= 65:
    print("You are entitled to a senior ticket")
else:
    print("Invalid age")
```

Output from program (when user enters "18") ✕

```
Please enter your age
18
Please purchase an adult ticket
```

Output from program (when user enters "-6") ✕

```
Please enter your age
-6
Invalid age
```

Example 26 – The "not" operator

▼ Program Code

```python
score = int(input("Please enter your score."))
if not(score == 76 or score == 58):
    print("You did not hit the target scores.")
else:
    print("Well done, target score achieved.")
```

Output from program (when user enters "58") ✕

```
Please enter your score.
58
Well done, target achieved.
```

A **not()** operator reverses the condition so rather than checking if the score entered is 76 or 58, the addition of the not means that the condition is only true if the score is not equal to 76 or 58.

This example can be used to highlight another fact about programming: often there are several ways to achieve the same outcome. By changing the highlighted code below, the program below will produce exactly the same results as example 26.

```
score = int(input("Please enter your score."))
if score == 76 or score == 58:
    print("Well done, target score achieved.")
else:
    print("You did not hit the target scores.")
```

Example 27 – Building more complex "if" statements

The complexity of the "if" statements you build is only limited by your own ability to work out the logic of the conditions. A more complex example is shown below:

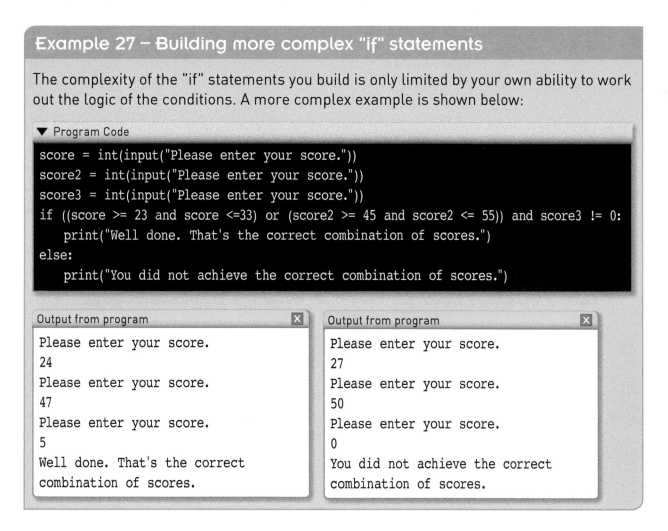

▼ Program Code

```
score = int(input("Please enter your score."))
score2 = int(input("Please enter your score."))
score3 = int(input("Please enter your score."))
if ((score >= 23 and score <=33) or (score2 >= 45 and score2 <= 55)) and score3 != 0:
    print("Well done. That's the correct combination of scores.")
else:
    print("You did not achieve the correct combination of scores.")
```

Output from program ☒

```
Please enter your score.
24
Please enter your score.
47
Please enter your score.
5
Well done. That's the correct
combination of scores.
```

Output from program ☒

```
Please enter your score.
27
Please enter your score.
50
Please enter your score.
0
You did not achieve the correct
combination of scores.
```

Chapter 12 – Computational thinking puzzles (if statements)

A good ability to predict the output from "if" commands will significantly improve your ability to design "if" statements and conditions of your own.

In the following questions you will be asked to predict the output from each small program using a variety of different inputs.

Example puzzle

```
number = int(input("Please enter an integer"))
if number < 10:
    print("Low")
if number >= 10 and number <= 20:
    print("Middle")
if number > 20:
    print("High")
```

> Remember: indented lines are only executed if the conditions are true.

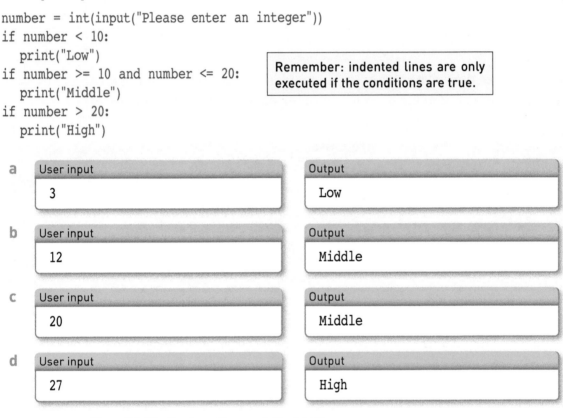

	User input	Output
a	3	Low
b	12	Middle
c	20	Middle
d	27	High

Puzzle set 5 – "If", "else" and "elif" statements

```
52 number = int(input("Enter a number to test the puzzle"))
    if number <= 50:
        print("Low")
    if number > 50 and number < 100:
        print("Middle")
    if number >= 100:
        print("High")
```

	User input	Output
a	23	
b	67	
c	100	

d
User input	Output
236	

e
User input	Output
50	

53
```
temp = int(input("Please enter a temperature"))
if temp >= -273 and temp <= 42:
    print("Solid")
elif temp >43 and temp < 87:
    print("Liquid")
else:
    print("Gas")
```

a
User input	Output
60	

b
User input	Output
–50	

c
User input	Output
43	

d
User input	Output
2999	

e Which of the above inputs (a, b, c or d) highlights an error in the logic of the program? Describe how you would correct the error in program.

54
```
age = int(input("Please enter an age"))
if age < 0 or age > 120:
    print("Age not valid")
else:
    print("Valid age")
    if age >= 3 and age <= 18:
        print("School age")
    if age >= 16:
        print("Working age")
    if age >= 60:
        print("Retirement age")
    if age >= 67:
        print("Pension age")
```

a

User input	Output from program
14	

b

User input	Output from program
–2	

c

User input	Output from program
47	

d   State an input that would output "Valid age", "School age" and "Working age".

55
```python
value = float(input("Please enter the value of your item"))
weight = float(input("Please enter the weight of your item in kilograms"))
if value <= 0:
   print("Invalid value")
   postage = 0.0
if weight >= 0 and weight < 2:
   if value > 0 and value < 50:
      postage = 1.5
   if value >= 50 and value < 150:
      postage = 2.75
   if value >= 150:
      postage = 5.5
elif weight >= 2 and weight < 10:
   if value > 0 and value < 50:
      postage = 2.5
   if value >= 50 and value < 150:
      postage = 4.4
   if value >= 150:
      postage = 8.35
elif weight >= 10 and weight < 25:
   if value > 0 and value < 50:
      postage = 7.55
   if value >= 50 and value < 150:
      postage = 12.3
   if value >= 150:
      postage = 15.0
else:
   postage = 25.0
print(postage)
```

a

User input	Value of postage displayed
value 62 weight 1.5	

b

User input	Value of postage displayed
value 0 weight 2.2	

c

User input	Value of postage displayed
value 172 weight 19	

d

User input	Value of postage displayed
value 250 weight 32.5	

e

User input	Value of postage displayed
value 34 weight 2.5	

f

User input	Value of postage displayed
value 50 weight 10	

56 The following program uses some of the string functions learned in Section 1. Beware, this is a difficult puzzle!

```
word = str(input("Please enter a word"))
number = int(input("Please enter an number"))
if len(word[number:]) >= 3:
  word = word + word
else:
  word = word[0:2] + word[0:2]
if word.count("e") >= 3:
  word = word.replace("e","a")
else:
  word = word.replace("e","c")
print(word)
```

a

User input	Value of "word" displayed
Please enter a word been Please enter a number 3	

b

User input	Value of "word" displayed
Please enter a word coffee Please enter a number 2	

c

User input	Value of "word" displayed
Please enter a word been Please enter a number 1	

Chapter 13 – Programming challenges for Section 2

Below is the next collection of programming challenges. For each challenge you are required to write Python code that includes selection (if) statements to solve the problem. Each of the problems involves using the Python statements, syntax and operators that you have learned in Section 2:

Statements and Syntax	Mathematical Operators	Logical Operators
• if • elif • else	• == • > • < • >= • <= • !=	• AND • OR • NOT

It's important that you don't forget what you learned earlier so each set of new challenges may also require you to use skills and knowledge from previous sections.

The challenges start off nice and easy but will get progressively harder.

Program challenges for selection statements

Program 20 – Advice please

Write a program that asks the user if they would like some advice. If they enter "Y", provide them with an amusing message.

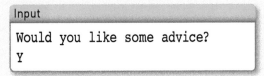
```
Input
Would you like some advice?
Y
```

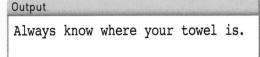
```
Output
Always know where your towel is.
```

Program 21 – Go winner

Go is a 4000-year-old board game played by two players using black and white stones. At the end of the game each player counts their score then white adds on an extra 6.5 points to make up for the fact they play second at the beginning of the game. The player with the highest score is the winner.

Write a program that asks black and white to enter their scores, adds on 6.5 points and displays the winner.

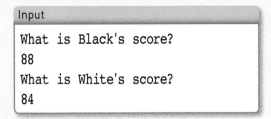
```
Input
What is Black's score?
88
What is White's score?
84
```

```
Output
After 6.5 is added the score is:
Black - 88
White - 90.5
White is the winner.
```

Program 22 – Charity collection

Three friends have been collecting money for charity. A local company has offered to double the amount of money they collect if they raise over £1000. Write a program that allows the friends to enter their individual amounts. The program should then add the three amounts and store the total. If the total is greater or equal to 1000 the total should be doubled. Finally, the total should be displayed.

Input	Output
Please enter the first amount raised. 398 Please enter the second amount raised. 193 Please enter the third amount raised. 478	A total of £1069 was raised. This will be doubled to £2138.

Program 23 – Calculate the area of a rectangle (part 2)

Program 5 asked you to calculate the area of a rectangle. Open this program and edit it to calculate the area of two rectangles. Once both areas have been calculated your program should decide which rectangle has the larger area and display a suitable message.

Input	Output
Rectangle 1 Please enter the length: 12 Please enter the width: 6 Rectangle 2 Please enter the length: 7 Please enter the width: 9	Rectangle 1 has the largest area

Program 24 – The most vowels

Write a program that asks the user to enter two sentences. The program should

- count the number of vowels in each sentence
- display the percentage of vowels, to 2 decimal places, in each sentence
  (percentage = 100 / number of letter in sentence * number of vowels)
- display the number of vowels in each sentence
- display which sentence has the most vowels.

Input	Output
Enter sentence 1 You can't handle the truth! Enter sentence 2 Houston, we have a problem.	The percentage of vowels in sentence 1 is: 25.93 The percentage of vowels in sentence 2 is: 33.33 Sentence 1 has 7 vowels. Sentence 2 has 9 vowels. Sentence 2 has more vowels.

Program 25 – Advice please (part 2)

Open and edit program 20 to include an alternative message if the user types "N". An error message should be given to the user if they enter anything other than "Y" or "N".

Input
Would you like some advice? D

Output
Sorry, you were asked to enter Y or N.

Program 26 – Car tyre check

As tyres wear out, it takes longer for a car to stop. At a given speed a car should be able to break and stop within the maximum recommended stopping distances shown.

Miles per hour	Recommended stopping distance(m)
30	14
50	38

Write a program to analyse the results of a braking test. The user should be asked to enter one of two speeds (30 or 50) and the distance it took the car to stop in the test. To allow for any measurement errors, the distance entered should be rounded up to the nearest whole number. Finally the user should be given a message stating if their car has:

- failed the tyre test – the car took longer than the recommended distance for the given speed to stop
- passed the test – the cars stopping distance was equal to or less than the recommended distance for the given speed.

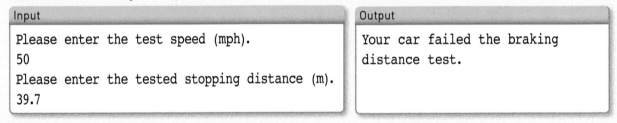

Input
Please enter the test speed (mph). 50 Please enter the tested stopping distance (m). 39.7

Output
Your car failed the braking distance test.

Program 27 – Charity collection (part 2)

The local company from Program 22 have decided that they cannot afford to double any amount of money raised over £1000. The following new decisions are made:

- any amount raised that is less than £1000 receives a £100 bonus
  (For example, £345 raised will result in £445 total)
- the company will still double the amount raised between £1000 and £2000
  (For example, £1282 raised will result in £2564 total)
- if the amount is over £2000, the initial £2000 is doubled but any additional money is not
  (For example, £2054 raised will result in 2 * £2000 + £54 = £4054 total)

Open and rewrite Program 22 to account for the above decisions.

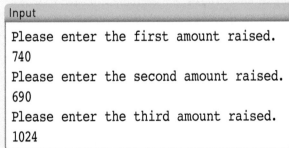

Input
Please enter the first amount raised. 740 Please enter the second amount raised. 690 Please enter the third amount raised. 1024

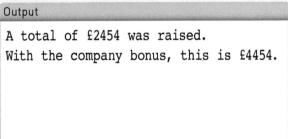

Output
A total of £2454 was raised. With the company bonus, this is £4454.

Section 3 – Repetition (loop) statements

An important aspect of programming is the ability to repeat lines of code. Imagine a design for a scientific survey program where the user is required to enter 1000 measurements.

Without the ability to repeat code, the same two lines of code (input the measurement, add the input to a total) would have to be copied and pasted 1000 times by the programmer. This would result in a very long program to carry out a fairly simple task (Figure 14.1).

Figure 14.2 shows the same design using repetition.

This design shows that when program code is repeated, an additional variable is required. In this example, the counter stores the number of times the repeated lines of code have been executed.

Instead of counting the number of repetitions, the user is asked if they wish to enter another measurement (shown in Figure 14.3).

An additional variable "choice" is required to store the user's input.

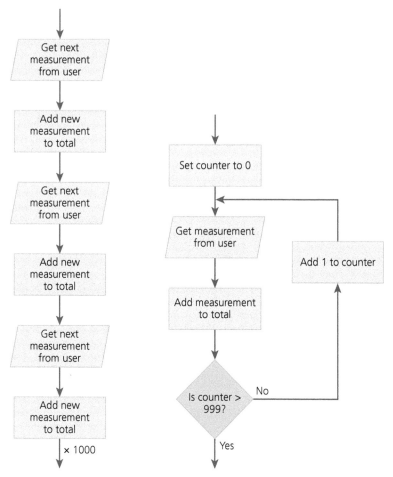

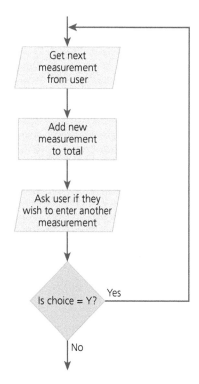

Figure 14.1: Adding measurements without repetition

Figure 14.2: Adding measurements using repetition

Figure 14.3: Adding measurements where user input ends repetition

Fixed and conditional loops

There are two types of repetition used in programming. Both are represented in Figures 14.2 and 14.3.

- **Fixed** loops – code is repeated a known number of times (for example, when we know that 1000 scientific measurements will be entered). This type of repetition is sometimes called '**count controlled**'.
- **Conditional** loops – code is repeated until certain conditions are met (for example, until the user does not enter "Y").

The type of loop you use in each program will be determined by one simple question.

Q: Do I know exactly how many times the code needs to be repeated?

A: Yes = fixed loop needed

    or

    No = conditional loop needed

Chapter 14 – Examples of repetition (loop) statements

Some examples of both types of loop in Python 3 are shown below. Try typing each of these programs into your Python editor and run them to see what happens.

Example 28 – A simple fixed loop

A fixed loop uses the **for** and **range( )** statements to state the number of times the code will be repeated. In this example the program loops four times.

▼ Program Code

```
for counter in range(4):
    print("This is a fixed loop.")
```

Output from program ☒

```
This is a fixed loop.
This is a fixed loop.
This is a fixed loop.
This is a fixed loop.
```

Note that loops are programming structures. Like an "if" statement, the "for" statement is followed by a colon and the lines below are indented to show that they are "inside" the loop.

Example 29 – A fixed loop with user input

In this example, the user is asked for input. The variable "times" has replaced the number in the range statement. The use of a variable allows the same program code to loop a different number of times. The user can now control the number of repetitions.

▼ Program Code

```
times = int(input("Enter a number"))
for counter in range(times):
    print("I must try harder.")
```

Output from program (when user enters "3") ☒

```
Enter a number
3
I must try harder.
I must try harder.
I must try harder.
```

This is another example of a fixed loop as the code still repeats a set number of times.

Example 30 – The loop variable

When a fixed loop executes, the program counts the number of times the code has been repeated. This count is stored in the loop variable, in this case 'money'. By displaying the loop variable using a print( ) statement we can see that range(5) will count from 0 and end at 4.

▼ Program Code

```
for money in range(5):
    print(money)
```

Output from program 🗙

```
0
1
2
3
4
```

Example 31 – More about the range( ) statement

The range( ) statement can be expanded to give two values: a **start** and **end** point for the count. This example also shows how the loop variable can be built into print( ) statements.

▼ Program Code

```
total = 0
print("Please enter the 3 test marks")
for counter in range(1,4):
    print("Please enter test",counter)
    mark = int(input())
    total = total + mark
print("The total number of marks =",total)
```

Output from program 🗙

```
Please enter the 3 test marks
Please enter test 1
13
Please enter test 2
17
Please enter test 3
6
The total number of marks = 36
```

Important note!

If a range of 1,4 is entered, the actual count is from 1 to 3 (one short of the second number in the range). Think of the second range value as when the loop should stop:

- 1 – execute the loop
- 2 – execute the loop
- 3 – execute the loop
- 4 – stop looping

Example 32 – Adding a step to the range( ) statement

If the range( ) statement contains only two values, the loop variable increments (increases) by 1 each time the loop executes.

If a third value is included in the range( ) statements the loop variable increments by this new value. So range(1,21,4) starts counting from 1 in **steps** of 4 each loop: 1 5 9 13 17. Note that the count doesn't include 21 as the loop stops executing before 21.

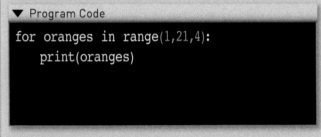

```
for oranges in range(1,21,4):
    print(oranges)
```

Output from program
```
1
5
9
13
17
```

A negative step would count down rather than up. In this case, the first number must be larger than the second.

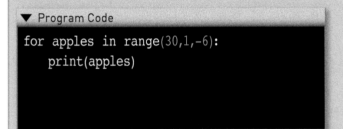

```
for apples in range(30,1,-6):
    print(apples)
```

Output from program
```
30
24
18
12
6
```

Example 33 – A conditional loop

Python uses the "while" statement to create a loop that will continually repeat when the conditions in the while command are true.

The complex condition choice! = "Y" and choice!= "N" can be read as:

"keep on looping while:
- the 'choice' variable is not equal to Y and
- the 'choice' variable is not equal to N".

▼ Program Code

```
choice = ""
while choice != "Y" and choice != "N":
    choice = str(input("Make your choice - Y/N."))
print("Thank you for making your choice.")
```

Output from program ☒

```
Make your choice - Y/N.
J
Make your choice - Y/N.
F
Make your choice - Y/N.
y
Make your choice - Y/N.
Y
Thank you for making your choice.
```

Conditions can often be written more than one way. How you write a condition may sometimes simply be personal preference based around how you visualise the code.

For example, the above condition could be rewritten as:

```
not(choice == "Y" or choice == "N")
```

This allows the programmer to write a condition stating the input you are looking for from the user (choice == "Y" or choice == "N") and then flip the complex condition using the not( ) operator. This method may be easier for you to design and code.

Example 34 – Input validation

Good programmers write code that prevent problems from occurring later in their programs.

A conditional (while) loop can be used to make sure that the user enters only valid input. This is important because invalid values may cause a program to crash (stop executing) or lead to invalid output (i.e. code not functioning correctly).

▼ Program Code

```
score = int(input("Please enter your score."))
while not(score >= 10 and score <= 20):
    print("Your score must be between 10 and 20 inclusive.")
    score = int(input("Please enter your score."))
```

Output from program ☒

```
Please enter your score.
34
Your score must be between 10 and 20 inclusive.
Please enter your score.
18
```

Well-written input validation code should include print( ) statements to produce a meaningful error message for the user if they enter invalid inputs. This ensures the user knows why their input was invalid.

Chapter 15 – Computational thinking puzzles (loops)

Visualising loops in your head can be quite tricky. In these puzzles, pay attention to the values in the range( ) statement and any values stored in variables.

You may wish to sketch out some working for these puzzles before you write down the output.

Puzzle set 6 – Fixed loops part 1

57
```
for counter in range(3):
    print("Graphics")
```
Output

58
```
for counter in range(1,3):
    print("Processor")
```
Output

59
```
type = "pug"
for dogs in range(5):
    print(type)
```
Output

60
```
for numbers in range(2,20,3):
    print(numbers)
```
Output

61
```
for listNums in range(10,55,10):
    print(listNums)
```
Output

62
```
for countdown in range(35,7,-5):
    print(countdown)
```
Output

63
```
number = 1
for countdown in range(4):
    number = number + 3
    print(number)
```
Output

A good understanding of the range( ) command is extremely helpful when designing and writing code with unconditional loops.

These puzzles are a bit different. This time you will be given the output and you must work out what is missing from the range( ) command.

For example:
```
for count in range(    ):
    print (count)
```
Output

0

4

8

12

To produce the output above, the missing range values:

- start counting from 0
- add on a step of 4 each time
- finish counting somewhere between 13 and 16
  (not 17 because that would lead to 16 also being displayed in the output).

Possible answers are therefore: range**(0,13,4)**, range**(0,14,4)**, range**(0,15,4)** or range**(0,16,4)**.

Using the same program used in the above example, write down the simplest range( ) that would produce the output shown.

Remember that a range( ) command can take three forms:

- range(5)
- range(2,7)
- range(1,20,4)

64

Range	Output from program
	0
	1
	2
	3
	4
	5

65

Range	Output from program
	2
	3
	4
	5

66

Range	Output from program
	7
	6
	5

67

Range	Output from program
	1
	4
	7
	10

68

Range	Output from program
	45
	36
	27
	18
	9

Puzzle set 7 – Trace tables

A trace table is a technique used to test the logical flow of programs without executing the code. The tester 'walks through' the program, manually calculating the values stored in variables at each stage of the program's execution.

Program code

```
num1 = 5
num2 = 7
for loop in range(4):
    num1 = num1 + num2
    num2 = num2 + 2
print(num1, num2)
```

Explanation

Each time the code repeats, num1 stores the current value of num1 + num2.

The value of num2 is then increased by 2.

This process is repeated four times "range(4)".

The two variables are displayed.

The trace table is used to note the values stored by the two variables after each repetition of the loop. This helps the programmer to identify mistakes in the logic of the code.

Trace table	num1	num2
beginning of program	5	7
after 1st loop	12	9
after 2nd loop	21	11
after 3rd loop	32	13
after last loop	45	15
final values displayed	45	15

On blank paper, sketch out a trace table to track the changing values of variables as you walk through the repeating code. Write down the final values of the variables that are displayed on the last line of each program.

69
```
num1 = 3
num2 = 2
for loop in range(3):
    num1 = num1 + num2
    num2 = num2 + 3
print(num1, num2)
```

Output

70
```
num1 = 80
num2 = 40
for loop in range(2):
    num1 = num1 - num2
    num2 = num2 / 2
print(num1, num2)
```

Output

71
```
num1 = 2
num2 = 4
num3 = 6
for loop in range(4):
    num1 = (num1 + num2 - 8) * 2
    num2 = num2 + num3
print(num1, num2, num3)
```

Output

72
```
num1 = 1
num2 = 3
num3 = 5
for loop in range(5):
    num3 = num1 + 3
    num2 = num3 - 2
    num1 = num3 + num2
print(num1, num2, num3)
```

Output

73
```
num1 = 5
num2 = 5
num3 = 5
for loop in range(200):
    num3 = num1 - (num2 + 2)
    num2 = (num2 - 2) - num3
    num3 = num3 + 7
print(num1, num2, num3)
```

Output

The loop variable will be used in the next few puzzles. Remember for range (3) the variable would store 0 then 1 then 2. For range(3,7) the variable would store: 3,4,5,6. For range(1,10,2) the variable would store 1,3,5,7,9.

74
```
num1 = 2
num2 = 4
for loop in range(4):
    num1 = num2 + num1
    num2 = num1 - loop
print(num1, num2)
```

Output

75
```
num1 = 4
num2 = 6
num3 = 0
for loop in range(3,7):
    num1 = (num1/2 + num2/3) * loop
    num3 = num2 + num1
print(int(num1), num2, int(num3))
```

Output

76
```
start = 1
for loop in range(1,6):
    start = start * 10
    mid = start%loop
    end = mid + loop
    start = end
print(start, mid, end)
```

Output

77 Remember about concatenation of strings using the + symbol. For example, "bob"+"cat" = "bobcat".

Follow the concatenation taking place in this puzzle and write down the string displayed in the final line.

```
text1 = "a"
text2 = "b"
text3 = ""
for loop in range(4):
    phrase1 = str(loop)+ text1
    phrase2 = text2 + str(loop)
    if loop <= 2:
        text3 = text3 + phrase1
    else:
        text3 = text3 + phrase2
print(text3)
```

Output

78 Now for a really difficult one, which combines a lot of what you have learned up to this point. Well done if you get this puzzle correct.

```
text1 = "this"
text2 = "is"
text3 = "hard"
words = ""
number = 0
for diamond in range(len(text2),len(text3)):
    words = words + text1 + text2
    number = number + words.count("s")
    words = words[2:5] + text3
    number = diamond + number + text3.count("h")
print(number)
```

Output

Puzzle set 8 – Conditional Loops

The next few puzzles will focus on understanding the conditions used in while loops.

Which of the input options (A, B, C or D) would end the conditional loop causing the "program finished" message to be displayed?

79
```
num = 0
while num!= 22:
    num = int(input("Please enter a number"))
print("program finished")
```

Answer

Input required to exit loop			
A	B	C	D
20	22	24	34

80
```
guess = 0
while not(guess == 34):
    guess = int(input("Please enter a number"))
print("program finished")
```

Answer

Input required to exit loop			
A	B	C	D
20	22	24	34

81
```
num = 34
while num == 34 or num == 22 or num == 20:
    num = int(input("Please enter a number"))
print("program finished")
```

Answer

Input required to exit loop			
A	B	C	D
20	22	24	34

82
```
temperature= 0
while temperature<= 45:
    temperature= int(input("Please enter a temperature"))
print("program finished")
```

Answer

Input required to exit loop			
A	B	C	D
–3	45	76	34

83
```
number = 0
while number < 5 or number > 17:
    number = int(input("Please enter a number"))
print("program finished")
```

Input required to exit loop			
A	B	C	D
17	45	–5	4

Answer

84
```
length = 0
while not(length >= 22 and length <=45):
    length = int(input("Please enter a length"))
print("program finished")
```

Input required to exit loop			
A	B	C	D
14	0	52	27

Answer

85
```
text = ""
while len(text) < 4:
    text = str(input("Please enter a word"))
print("program finished")
```

Input required to exit loop			
A	B	C	D
say	hello	bye	3

Answer

86
```
word = ""
while word.count("s") < 2:
    word = str(input("Please enter a word"))
print("program finished")
```

Input required to exit loop			
A	B	C	D
s	loser	loss	slate

Answer

87
```
text = ""
while text.count("a") <=1 or len(text) < 4:
    text = str(input("Please enter a word"))
print("program finished")
```

Input required to exit loop			
A	B	C	D
afar	blast	aga	ta

Answer

Chapter 16 – Programming challenges for Section 3

The next collection of programming challenges involve repeating code using fixed and conditional loops. For each challenge you are required to write Python code that includes repetition statements to solve the problem. Each of the problems involves using the Python statements, syntax and operators that you have learned in Section 3:

Statements and Syntax	Variations
● for	● range(4)
● range( )	● range(2,6)
● while	● range(1, 50,5)

As always, these new challenges may also require you to use skills and knowledge from previous sections. The challenges start off nice and easy but will get progressively harder.

Program challenges for repetition (fixed loop) statements

Program 28 – Lines cheat

A naughty student has been given lines to copy as a punishment from their Computing teacher. They have been asked to type out "Don't behave like a muppet in class." 20 times. Write a program that asks a student to enter a sentence. The same sentence should then be displayed 20 times.

```
Input
Which sentence would you like copied?
Don't behave like a muppet in class.
```

```
Output
Don't behave like a muppet in class.
Don't behave like a muppet in class.
Don't behave like a muppet in class.
        … displayed 20 times in total
```

Program 29 – Charity collection (part 3)

Open and edit Program 27. The final total should be displayed 3 times to emphasise the amount of money raised.

```
Input
Please enter the first amount raised.
398
Please enter the second amount raised.
193
Please enter the third amount raised.
478
```

```
Output
A total of £1069 was raised.
This will be doubled to:
£2138!!!
£2138!!!
£2138!!!
```

Program 30 – Name switch

An artist has been experimenting with making electronic art from names. Their first attempt involves creating a pattern out of a first name and surname. Write a program that asks for two names to be input and then displays the exact pattern shown in the output using substring, concatenation, upper and lower.

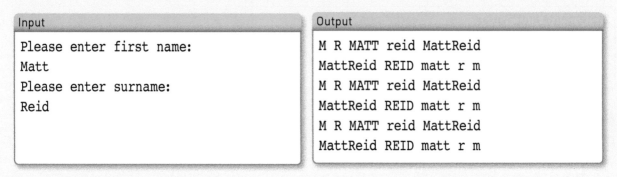

```
Input
Please enter first name:
Matt
Please enter surname:
Reid
```

```
Output
M R MATT reid MattReid
MattReid REID matt r m
M R MATT reid MattReid
MattReid REID matt r m
M R MATT reid MattReid
MattReid REID matt r m
```

Program 31 – Cricket over

In cricket, a team bowls six balls in an "over". Write a program that allows six scores to be entered, one for each ball in the over. The total scored in that over should then be displayed.

(If you know cricket, you'll know that an over is not always six balls but for the purposes of this program we will assume that it is.)

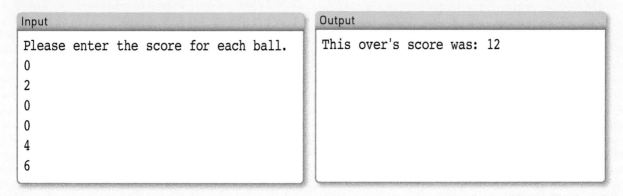

```
Input
Please enter the score for each ball.
0
2
0
0
4
6
```

```
Output
This over's score was: 12
```

Program 32 – Average temperature

A weather experiment is set up to calculate the average temperature on a mountain peak during the course of a week. The following measurements are taken at 1pm every day.

Mon 12°C   Tue 14°C   Wed 7°C   Thur 6°C   Fri 7°C   Sat 11°C   Sun 11°C

A program needs to be created to allow the user to enter the seven temperatures.
The average for the week should be displayed, to two decimal places, as shown below.

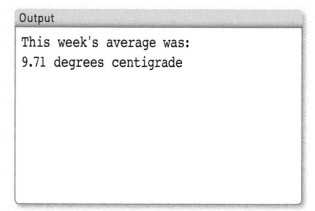

Program 33 – Lines cheat (part 2)

The pupil from Program 28 forgot to hand their lines in and now has more to do. Open and edit Program 28 to allow the pupil to select how many lines the program displays.

Input
Which sentence would you like copied?
Mr Reid is the best teacher.
How many times would you like this copied?
54

Output
Mr Reid is the best teacher.
Mr Reid is the best teacher.
...displayed 54 times in total

Program 34 – Charity collection (part 4)

The following year, the three friends recruit many more charity raisers. Open and edit Program 29 to ask for the number of people raising money to be entered. The program will then total up the money raised by the group and display the output as before in Program 29.

Input
How many charity raisers were there?
6
Enter the total raised by each:
238
624
546
333
651
174

Output
A total of £2566 was raised.
This will be increased to:
£4566!!!
£4566!!!
£4566!!!

Program 35 – Press up challenge

Naebor High School have organised a fitness challenge. Each school records the time it takes each student to do 50 press ups. Write a program that asks a user to enter the number of students taking part and the time (in seconds) for each student, as shown below (note that the students are numbered). The program should then display the average time for all the students (to 2 decimal places).

```
Input

Please enter the number of students:
3
Enter the time in seconds for each student.
Student 1
82
Student 2
67
Student 3
45
```

```
Output

The average time for the 3 students was:
64.67 seconds
```

Program 36 – Number patterns

A math teacher shows her class a list of odd numbers, explaining that the pattern starts at 1 and then misses out every second number. Write a program to display the list of odd numbers shown below.

```
Output

Odd Numbers List
1
3
5
7
9
11
```

Program 37 – Number pattern (part 2)

Open and edit Program 36 so that the user can choose the first and last odd numbers displayed. This problem is slightly harder than it looks.

Input	Output
The following program will display odd numbers. Enter the first number in the list 5 Enter the last number in the list 13	Odd Numbers List 5 7 9 11 13

Program challenges for repetition (conditional loop) statements

Program 38 – Password

A program is required to continually ask a user to enter a password until it has been entered correctly. The program should give the user an error message if they enter the wrong password. A message "Entry gained!" should be displayed when the password in entered correctly. You may choose the password.

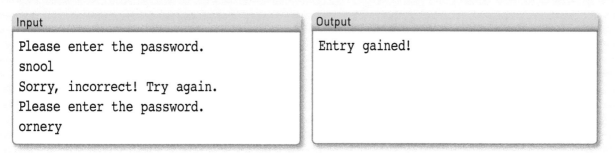

Input	Output
Please enter the password. snool Sorry, incorrect! Try again. Please enter the password. ornery	Entry gained!

Program 39 – Number pattern (part 3)

Open Program 37. Add input validation to the program that ensures the second number entered by the user is more than the first number + 20.

Input	Output
The following program will display odd numbers. Enter the first number in the list 5 Enter the last number in the list 17 Sorry, the number must be at least 5+20 Please re-enter the number 27	Odd Numbers List 5 7 9 11 13 15 17 19 21 23 25

Program 40 – Advice please (part 3)

You have decided that your user definitely requires some advice. Open and edit program 25 so that it will continue to ask if your user wants advice until they enter "Y". Include an amusing message if they enter "N" and an error message if they don't enter "Y" or "N".

Input	Output
Would you like some advice? H Please enter Y or N only. Would you like some advice? N Don't be silly. You definitely need advice! Would you like some advice? Y	Don't feed the trolls!

Program 41 – No more presents

You have £200 to spend on your birthday. Write a program that will ask you to enter the price of each present on your wish list until your total is over £200. The program should produce the output shown.

Input	Output
Please enter the price of each present: 35 100 50 45	Limit Exceeded. You can't include the £45 present.

Program 42 – Menu system

An input validation is required for a larger program where users press a key to select an option. Write the code required to ensure a user can only enter the letters: Q, A, K or L.

The program should accept both upper and lower case versions of each letter. An error message should be displayed if the user enters an invalid letter. The program should also display a message when a valid letter is entered.

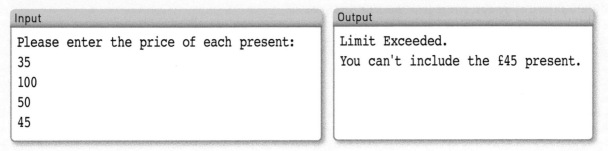

Input and Output (run 1)	Input and Output (run 2)
Enter your menu choice (Q, A, K or L) a A selected	Enter your menu choice (Q, A, K or L) V V is not valid. Enter Q, A, K or L L L selected

Difficult program challenges for repetition (loop) statements

The following challenges are designed to be difficult. Break each problem down into small stages. Test each part of the program as you write it. It's easier to find errors in a couple of new lines than in an entire program. Congratulate yourself if you manage to complete any of the tasks.

Program 43 – Guess the number

A simple game is required where a user tries repeatedly to guess an unknown number between 1 and 100. Each time the user guesses, the program should:

- check that the input is an integer between 1 and 100
- inform the user if their guess is too high, too low or correct.

The guessing game only finishes when the user's guess matches the unknown number. An example of the program running (input and output) is shown below.

```
Input and Output
Guess the hidden number between 1 and 100.
Enter your guess.
112
Your guess was not valid. Enter it again.
67
Your guess is too high. Try again.
50
Your guess is too low. Try again.
52
Correct! Well Done.
```

Program 44 – Average temperature (part 2)

Open and edit Program 32 to ensure each input is between −40°C and 55°C and that the program displays the week's average temperature for 4 weeks. The average for each week should then be displayed as shown below.

```
Input
Week 1
Please enter the seven temperatures.
12
14
7
6
66
Temperature should be between -40 and 55
7
11
11
Week 2
           ...and so on for all 4 weeks
```

```
Output
Week 1 average was:
9.71 degrees centigrade
Week 2 average was:
11.25 degrees centigrade
Week 3 average was:
10.03 degrees centigrade
Week 4 average was:
14.28 degrees centigrade
```

Program 45 – Pailwater darts tournament

Jack and Jill are competing in the annual Pailwater darts competition. Each competitor throws three rounds of darts. The entry for each individual round should be validated to ensure the user has entered a valid darts score (between 0 and 180). The player with the highest individual round score is the winner.

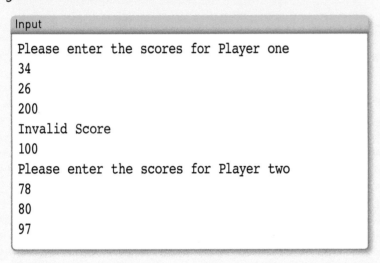

```
Input
Please enter the scores for Player one
34
26
200
Invalid Score
100
Please enter the scores for Player two
78
80
97
```

```
Output
Player one scored the highest individual score.
Player one wins!!
```

Section 4 – Storing multiple values using lists

If you look carefully at the examples, puzzles and problems in Sections 1 to 3, you will find that they all use simple variables to store single strings or numbers. Variables are appropriate where your program only stores single values, for example, a total or a person's surname.

1D List

Where multiple values need to be stored (say, 1000 temperature readings taken from a sensor), we need a larger data structure called an **array**. An array holds data in indexed **elements**. The program uses the array name and index to determine where data should be stored or where it should be fetched from.

index	name
0	Omar
1	Jill
2	Derek
3	Ploy
4	Brad
5	Jessie

For example, print(name[3]) would display "Ploy".

Note that while Python can create arrays (you can download and install a module library called **NumPy**), for the purposes of learning how to use arrays we will use Python's **list structure**. While these are not truly arrays, for beginners, lists behave in a similar way. You may wish to research the difference between lists and arrays when you have completed this book.

As shown above, a list can be visualised as a column of **indexed** (numbered) boxes.

When **initialising** (creating) a list in a program, the programmer must enter:

- the name of the list
- the size of the list (number of elements/boxes)

The command for **declaring** an empty list in Python looks like this:

For a list of 6 numbers:	For a list of 10 strings:
`teamScores = [0]*6`	`teamNames = [""]*10`

index	teamScores
0	0
1	0
2	0
3	0
4	0
5	0

index	teamNames
0	
1	
2	
3	
4	
5	
6	
8	
8	
9	

2D list

Programmers sometimes use lists structures with more than one dimension. These are useful when the data being stored takes the form of a table or rectangular grid. A 2D list has two indexes which work like coordinates to identify a single element in the list.

artists

first index	second index 0	1	2
0	Andy	Warhol	Pop Art
1	Pablo	Picasso	Cubism
2	Leonardo	da Vinci	Renaissance

The string "Cubism" is stored in element 1,2.

Python lists can be used to implement a structure similar to a 2D list by creating sub lists within a main list.

To create the 2D list shown above, we first create the main list. Each element of the main list will store all of the information on one artist. Next we create a **sublist** of three elements to store the forename, surname and artistic style for one artist. This sublist is stored inside one element of the main list.

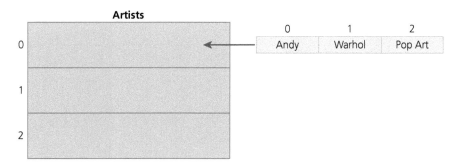

Figure 15.1: Sublist creation

A new sublist is created for each artist until the final structure looks like this:

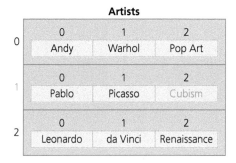

Figure 15.2: Final 2d list structure

A single element of the list of lists structure is accessed using the index of the main list and the index of the sublist.

```
print(artists[1][2])
```

This print statement would display Cubism.

Chapter 17 – Examples of lists

Example 35 – Adding values to a list

The elements of a Python list are numbered from 0 onwards. This index system is used by the programmer to select which of the list's elements they are going to store a value in.

To create a list of five integers and then store values in elements 2 and 4, we could write the code below.

```
points = [0]*5
points[2] = 23
points[4] = 49
```

index	points
0	0
1	0
2	23
3	0
4	49

As the numbering of the elements in a list starts at 0, index 2 would actually be the third element. Elements will continue to store the original value of 0 until this is changed by a new value being stored. After the above code is executed, three elements still store 0.

Example 36 – Initialising a list with different values

The elements of a list do not have to be given the value 0 or null ("") when the list is **initialised** (created).

If you wish to begin your program with a list of stored data, say ten names and ages, this could be done as shown below.

▼ Program Code

```
names = ["Azil","Gillian","Brian","Kuba","Jean","Doreen","Kye","Pat","Dennis","Ann"]
ages  = [13,14,13,15,16,13,14,14,14,13]
```

Example 37 – Output from a list using loops

To display all the names and ages in the previous example we could add the following code to the program.

▼ Program Code

```
print(names[0],ages[0])
print(names[1],ages[1])
print(names[2],ages[2])
print(names[3],ages[3])
print(names[4],ages[4])
print(names[5],ages[5])
print(names[6],ages[6])
print(names[7],ages[7])
print(names[8],ages[8])
print(names[9],ages[9])
```

Output from program

```
Azil 13
Gillian 14
Brian 13
Kuba 15
Jean 16
Doreen 13
Kye 14
Pat 14
Dennis 14
Ann 13
```

Although the previous code works, it is a poor solution. If our lists held 1000 names and ages we would need to write 1000 print commands.

As the print command is being repeated, a simpler solution would be to use a loop.

▼ Program Code

```
names = ["Azil","Gillian","Brian","Kuba","Jean","Doreen","Kye","Pat","Dennis","Ann"]
ages = [13,14,13,15,16,13,14,14,14,13]
for counter in range(10):
    print( names[counter], ages[counter] )
```

The program now has only one print( ) statement. The loop variable 'counter' is used to change the index of the list element being displayed. Counter will increment by one each time the loop repeats. This will produce the same output as before.

Note that by using the len( ) function we don't even need to know how many elements are in our list. The following code would work for any length of list.

▼ Program Code

```
names = ["Azil","Gillian","Brian","Kuba","Jean","Doreen","Kye","Pat","Dennis","Ann"]
ages = [13,14,13,15,16,13,14,14,14,13]
for counter in range(len(names)):
    print( names[counter], ages[counter] )
```

Example 38 – Input into a list using fixed and conditional loops

A fixed or conditional loop may also be used to input multiple values and store them in different elements of a list.

Fixed loop

Used when we know how many values the user is going to enter.

▼ Program Code

```
names = [""]*5
ages = [0]*5
for counter in range(5):
    names[counter] = str(input("Please enter name " + str(counter+1)))
    ages[counter] = int(input("Please enter " + names[counter] + "'s age"))
```

Input and output from program   ☒

```
Please enter name 1 Azil
Please enter Azil's age 13
Please enter name 2 Gillian
Please enter Gillian's age 14
Please enter name 3 Brian
Please enter Brian's age 13
Please enter name 4 Kuba
Please enter Kuba's age 15
Please enter name 5 Jean
Please enter Jean's age 16
```

The program uses the counter variable to ensure that each time a name and age are entered by the user they are stored in different elements of the list.

index	name
0	Azil
1	Gillian
2	Brian
3	Kuba
4	Jean

index	age
0	13
1	14
2	13
3	15
4	16

1st loop, counter = 0

2nd loop, counter = 1

3rd loop, counter = 2

4th loop, counter = 3

5th loop, counter = 4

Note that the second input line uses the name that was just entered by the user. This provides a clearer message for the user. It is always good practice to make your program as easy to use as possible.

Conditional loop

Used when we don't know how many values will be entered.

▼ Program Code

```
names = [""]*0
ages = [0]*0
counter = 0
morePeople = "Y"
while morePeople.lower() == "y":
    names.append(str(input("Please enter name " + str(counter+1))))
    ages.append(int(input("Please enter " + names[counter] + "'s age")))
    morePeople = str(input("Do you wish to enter more? Y/N"))
    if morePeople.lower() != "y":
        print("Entry complete")
    else:
        counter = counter + 1
```

A conditional loop allows data to be input until the user decides to stop. It requires the following additions:

- We start by initialising the lists with no elements because we don't know the size of the final lists. The **append( )** function is used to add a new element to the list making it grow in size with each new input.
- We need a way of controlling whether or not the while loop will repeat or finish. We can use another variable (**morePeople**) and an input ("Do you wish to enter more? Y/N") to do this.

Example 39 – Adding null values to a list of lists (2D list structure)

An empty list of lists can be created using the following code.

▼ Program code (null strings)

```
members = [ [""] * 2 for main in range(3) ]
```

▼ Program code (integers)

```
members = [ [0] * 5 for main in range(5) ]
```

▼ Program code (floats)

```
members = [ [0.0] * 100 for main in range(100) ]
```

The above code uses a variation of a fixed loop to create a single sublist and then repeat this multiple times.

Looking at the example below:
- The first number (5) is the value being stored in every element of the 2D list.
- The second number in the code (4) creates the number of elements in the sub list.
- The last number in the range( ) equals the number of main list elements.
  ```
  gridPoints = [[5] * 4 for main in range(2)]
  ```

This would create:

gridPoints	second index			
first index	0	1	2	3
0	5	5	5	5
1	5	5	5	5

Example 40 – Adding data to a list of lists (2D list structure)

A 2D list can be initialised (created) with data already stored in each element.

▼ Program code

```
artists = [ ["Andy","Warhol","Pop Art"], ["Pablo","Picasso","Cubism"], ["Leonardo","da
Vinci","Renaissance"] ]
```

▼ Program code

```
scores = [ [78,72,76,89,77], [90,88,70,73,74] ]
```

Example 41 – Adding user input to a list of lists (2D list structure)

If the sublist length is relatively small, user input can be stored using one loop and a small number of input statements.

▼ Program code (small sublist)

```
members = [[""] * 2 for main in range(3)]
for people in range(3):
    members[people][0]=str(input("Please enter the forename of person, people"))
    members[people][1]=str(input("Please enter the surname of person, people"))
for people in range(3):
    print(members[people][0],members[people][1])
```

If the sublist is longer, a nested loop may be required for the second index. This would be more efficient than repeating the input statements many, many times.

The program below allows the user to input a temperature every hour for a whole week.

▼ Program code (larger sublist)

```
temperature = [[0.0] * 24 for main in range(7)]
for day in range(7):
    for hour in range(24):
        temperature[day][hour]=float(input("Enter the next temperature"))
```

When the nested loop first executes, the two loop variables store day = 0 and hour = 0. While day remains at 0, the inner loop will count from hour = 0 up to hour = 23. When the inner loop finishes the outer loop will repeat and day will increment (day = 1). The inner loop then repeats another 24 times (0 to 23). This process repeats until all 168 (7 outer loops and 24 inner loops) list elements store a temperature.

The 2D list will be filled with temperatures one row at a time.

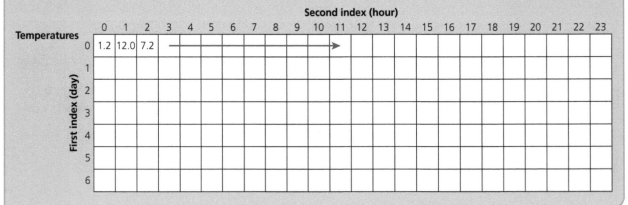

Example 42 – Outputting a list of lists (2D list structure) in rows and columns

▼ Program code

```
temperature = [[0.0] * 24 for main in range(7)]
for day in range(7):
    for hour in range(24):
    temperature[day][hour]=float(input("Enter the next temperature"))
for day in range(7):
    for hour in range(24):
        print(temperature[day][hour],"",end=' ')
    print()
```

This example displays the data in example 42 in rows and columns. The **end=' '** statement forces the next print statement to continue to output on the same line (when normally print statements output onto a new line). For the inner loop (hour), this means that each of the temperatures will be displayed next to each other. A space character "" is added to the output to separate the values.

The purpose of the empty print( ) statement is to cancel the effect of the 'end' statement each time the outer loop (day) increments.

Using this simple technique, the output can be displayed on 7 lines, each with 24 temperatures. Without the additional code all 168 temperatures would display vertically with each on its own line.

Chapter 18 – Computational thinking puzzles (lists)

The first set of puzzles in this chapter is designed to get you used to thinking of a list as a set of numbered elements.

In each set of puzzles a list is initialised and then values are assigned to elements of the list. Your task is to work out what values will be stored in each list element when the program has finished running.

For example:

```
numbers = [2]*5
numbers[3] = 4
numbers[0] = 1
```

index	points
0	1
1	2
2	2
3	4
4	2

Explanation
There are three lines of code:

1 numbers = [2]*5   All 5 elements are assigned the value 2

2 numbers[3] = 4   Change element 3 to 4

3 numbers[0] = 1   Change element 0 to 1

Puzzle set 9 – Assigning values to lists

The next few puzzles will focus on understanding how values are assigned to different indexes in a list.

88
```
numbers = [0]*5
numbers[2] = 33
numbers[4] = 22
numbers[3] = 11
```

	numbers
0	
1	
2	
3	
4	

89
```
numbers = [9]*5
numbers[0] = 5
numbers[2] = 9
numbers[4] = 0
```

	numbers
0	
1	
2	
3	
4	

90
```
numbers = [0,1,2,3,4]
numbers[1] = 4
numbers[4] = 1
numbers[3] = 2
```

numbers
0
1
2
3
4

91
```
numbers = [5]*5
numbers[2] = 2*4
numbers[4] = 20/2
numbers[3] = 6+6
numbers[2] = 5
```

numbers
0
1
2
3
4

92
```
numbers = [12,2,24,4,36]
numbers[2] = 3
numbers[4] = numbers[2]
numbers[2] = 6
numbers[1] = 20 + numbers[3] - numbers[2]
```

numbers
0
1
2
3
4

93
```
import math
numbers = [5]*5
numbers[3] = math.ceil(numbers[1]*3/2) - 3
numbers[0] = pow(numbers[3],2) - 16
numbers[4] = int(numbers[0] / 4)
```

numbers
0
1
2
3
4

94
```
numbers = [10]*5
numbers[2] = numbers[1] + 15
numbers[3] = numbers[0] - 5
if numbers[2] + numbers[4] >= 35:
  numbers[0] = numbers[0] + 10
else:
    numbers[0] = numbers[0] - 10
if numbers[0]%2 == 1:
    numbers[4] = numbers[3] + 2
else:
    numbers[4] = numbers[0] + 10
```

	numbers
0	
1	
2	
3	
4	

95
```
numbers = [0]*5
for nums in range(5):
    numbers[nums] = 3
```

	numbers
0	
1	
2	
3	
4	

96
```
numbers = [0]*5
counter = 0
for loop in range(5):
    numbers[loop] = counter
    counter = counter + 1
```

	numbers
0	
1	
2	
3	
4	

97
```
numbers = [0]*5
for loop in range(5):
    numbers[loop] = loop
```

	numbers
0	
1	
2	
3	
4	

98
```
numbers = [2]*5
for loop in range(4):
    numbers[loop +1] = numbers[loop] + loop + 1
```

	numbers
0	
1	
2	
3	
4	

99
```
wordLength = [0]*5
words = ["silly","humorous","funny","side-splitting","amusing"]
for loop in range(5):
    wordLength[loop] = len(words[loop])
```

	wordLength
0	
1	
2	
3	
4	

Puzzle set 10 – More than one list

As your programs grow in complexity you will naturally become better at understanding increasingly longer sections of code. Let's put a few concepts together again, this time using more programs with two lists!

100 What names will be stored in the two lists once the program has been executed?
```
nameList1 = ["Bob","Derek","Fred","Usman","Abubakar"]
nameList2 = ["Mary","Nida","Jill","Tracy","Helen"]
for loop in range(5):
    nameList1[loop] = nameList2[loop]
```

	nameList1			nameList2
0			0	
1			1	
2			2	
3			3	
4			4	

101
```
townList1 = ["Dover","Maidstone","Ayr","Shepway","Pembroke"]
townList2 = [""]*5
for loop in range(5):
    townList2[loop] = townList1[loop].lower()
```

	townList1			townList2
0			0	
1			1	
2			2	
3			3	
4			4	

102
```
places = ["Glasgow","Swansea","Lisburn","Thurso","Bolton"]
letterCount = [0]*5
for loop in range(5):
    letterCount[loop] = places[loop].count("o")
```

	places			letterCount
0			0	
1			1	
2			2	
3			3	
4			4	

103 What is stored in the "elements" list after the program has been executed?
```
elements = ["Copper","Titanium","Iron","Lead","Silicon"]
for loop in range(5):
    if elements[loop].count("i") > 1:
        elements[loop] = elements[4-loop]
```

	elements
0	
1	
2	
3	
4	

104 This contains part of a well-known algorithm. Work out what is stored in the numbers list after the loop has finished executing.
```
numbers = [45,9,35,92,67]
temporary = 0
for loop in range(4):
    if numbers[loop] > numbers[loop+1]:
        temporary = numbers[loop]
        numbers[loop] = numbers[loop+1]
        numbers[loop+1] = temporary
```

	numbers
0	
1	
2	
3	
4	

105 This puzzle uses substring (nameList1[loop][0:1]) to extract part of the stored strings for a list. If you can't remember how sub strings work, you can look back at Section 1. What strings will be stored in the two lists once the program has been executed?
```
nameList1 = ["Bob","Derek","Fred","Usman","Abubakar"]
nameList2 = ["Mary","Nida","Jill","Tracy","Helen"]
temporary = ""
for names in range(5):
    if nameList1[names][0:1] < nameList2[names][0:1]:
        temporary = nameList1[names ]
        nameList1[names] = nameList2[names]
        nameList2[names] = temporary
```

	nameList1			nameList2
0			0	
1			1	
2			2	
3			3	
4			4	

106 What values would be stored in the "values" list after this program has executed?

```
values = [45.78, 12.34, 102.14, 5.26, 1034.99]
temp1 = 0
for num in range(5):
    temp1 = values[num] - int(values[num])
    values[num] = int(temp1*10)
```

	values
0	
1	
2	
3	
4	

107 Last one, so let's make it difficult! Follow the logic of the code and work out what will be stored in the two lists after the program has executed.

```
import math
firstValue = [7.7, 3.2, 5.2, 6.4, 8.9]
secondValue = [9, 6, 4, 12, 10]
for num in range(5):
    if round(firstValue[num]) > firstValue[num]:
        secondValue[num] = secondValue[num] * math.ceil(firstValue[num])
    else:
        secondValue[num] = secondValue[num] * math.ceil(firstValue[num]) / 2
    if secondValue[num] > 50:
        firstValue[num] = 99
    else:
        firstValue[num] = 0
```

	firstValue
0	
1	
2	
3	
4	

	secondValue
0	
1	
2	
3	
4	

Puzzle set 11 – 2D lists

A program is written to store the following data in a list of lists.

```
words = [ ["Great","lives","significantly","SET","today"],
["Hsin","Watch","onto","the","is"], ["affect","everyone","else","BAR","open"],
["match","be","ready","high","should"], ["sure","off","The","sunny","Make"],
["you're","Gillian","eagerly","stepped","outside"] ]
```

words

first index	0	1	2	3	4
0	Great	lives	significantly	SET	today
1	Hsin	Watch	onto	the	is
2	affect	everyone	else	BAR	open
3	match	be	ready	high	should
4	sure	off	The	sunny	Make
5	you're	Gillian	eagerly	stepped	outside

second index

For the following puzzles, state the output if the following code was added to the above program.

108 `print(words[1][0],words[5][3],words[5][4])`

Output

109 `print(words[4][2], words[3][0], words[1][4], words[4][1], words[0][4])`

Output

110 `print(words[4][4].lower())`

Output

111 This puzzle uses substring to extract characters from the words in the 2D list.
`print(words[0][3][0:1] + words[0][3][1:].lower())`

Output

112 `for second in range(1,5):`
    `print(words[5][second])`

Output

113 `for first in range(0,4):`
    `print(words[first][3].lower(),"",end='')`

Output

114 `for first in range(0,4,2):`
    `for second in range(3):`
        `print(words[first][second],"",end='')`

Output

For the remaining puzzles in this set the following program was written.

```
grid = [ [5,8,6], [3,4,5], [6,1,0] ]
```

grid		second index	
first index	0	1	2
0	5	8	6
1	3	4	5
2	6	1	0

If the code in the following questions was added to the above code state the output.

115
```
for first in range(3):
    print(grid[first][0]+grid[first][1]+grid[first][2])
```

Output

116
```
if (grid[0][1]/grid[1][1]) == 2:
    print(grid[2][1])
else:
    print(grid[2][2])
```

Output

117
```
for first in range(len(grid)-1):
    for second in range(3):
        print(grid[first][second],end='')
    print()
```

Output

118
```
total = 0
grid[2][2] = 2
grid[0][2] = 3
grid[0][1] = grid[1][2]
for first in range(3):
    for second in range(3):
        total = total + grid[first][second]
print(total)
```

Output

119 This difficult puzzle displays all nine integers but what order are they displayed in?
```
for second in range(2,-1,-1):
    for first in range(2,-1,-1):
        print(grid[first][second],end='')
    print()
```

Output

Chapter 19 – Programming challenges for Section 4

The next collection of programming challenges are all about using Python lists to store multiple values. When you are writing programs that use values stored in lists you will nearly always use a loop to retrieve and use the stored information. The syntax covered in Section 4 was:

Statements and Syntax	Examples
• [ ] **Indexing List Elements** • [0] • [0,0] or • [loop] • [outerLoop,innerLoop]	• text[6].lower( ) • text[3][0:3] • int(number[5]) • round(number[2],2) • print(translation[0,0],"=",translation[0,1])

Program challenges for lists

Program 46 – For sale

A program is required to display a list of five items for sale on a monitor. Assign five sale items to a new list and then display these items as output.

```
Output

Mountain Bike
Ski Jacket
Electric Guitar
PS3 - 500Gb
Badminton Racquet
```

Program 47 – For sale (part 2)

Edit the above program to store a second list of five prices, one for each of the sale items. Display both the name and price of each sale item on the same line.

```
Output

Mountain Bike - £200
Ski Jacket - £67
Electric Guitar - £330
PS3 - 500Gb - £120
Badminton Racquet - £15
```

Program 48 – Cricket over (part 2)

Open and edit Program 31. Each time the user enters the score for one of the six balls it should be stored in a list. Display the messages shown in the output below along with the six scores entered by the user.

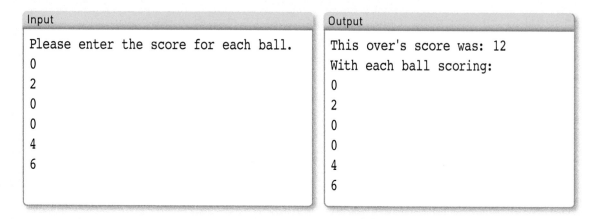

Input	Output
Please enter the score for each ball. 0 2 0 0 4 6	This over's score was: 12 With each ball scoring: 0 2 0 0 4 6

Program 49 – Dance group

Write a program to store the names and ages of four competitors in a dance competition. The program should display the competitor's name along with their competition level. Junior competitors are less than 12 years old, Senior competitors are at least 18 years old. Teen competitors are aged 12–17.

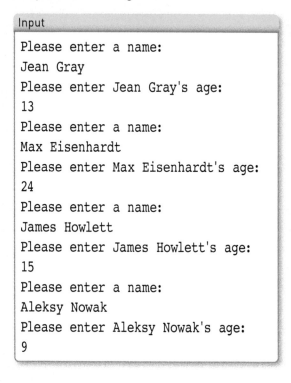

Input	Output
Please enter a name: Jean Gray Please enter Jean Gray's age: 13 Please enter a name: Max Eisenhardt Please enter Max Eisenhardt's age: 24 Please enter a name: James Howlett Please enter James Howlett's age: 15 Please enter a name: Aleksy Nowak Please enter Aleksy Nowak's age: 9	Names and Competition List: Jean Gray - Teen Max Eisenhardt - Senior James Howlett - Teen Aleksy Nowak - Junior

Program 50 – Horse hands

A computer program stores the names, ages and heights of ten horses in a riding school. (Note that the height of horses is measured in "hands" – usually a number between 6 and 18.) The user of the program will be asked to select a horse by entering a maximum age and height of the horse they wish to ride. All the horses with an age and height less than or equal to the user's input should be displayed as shown in the output.

Input
```
Please enter details of your horse.
Maximum height:
16
Maximum age:
15
```

Output
```
Suitable horses are:
Black Beauty, 14 years, 15 hands
Francine, 8 years, 14 hands
Langrish, 15 years, 14 hands
```

Program 51 – House size

The size of a house is calculated by adding together the floor area of each room. Write a program that asks the user how many rooms are in a house. The program should ask for the name, length and width of each room in turn before storing the name and area (to 1 decimal place) of each room. The program should then display the information below for the house.

Input
```
House floor area calculator.
Please enter the number of rooms:
3
Please enter the name of room 1: Lounge
Please enter the length (m) of room 1: 3.56
Please enter the width (m) of room 1: 4.7
Please enter the name of room 2: Kitchen
Please enter the length (m) of room 2: 2.26
Please enter the width (m) of room 2: 3.69
Please enter the name of room 3: Bedroom
Please enter the length (m) of room 3: 4.5
Please enter the width (m) of room 3: 4.7
```

Output
```
House details:
Room - Lounge
16.7 metres squared
Room - Kitchen
8.3 metres squared
Room - Bedroom
21.2 metres squared
The total area is calculated as:
46.2 metres squared
```

Program 52 – Who's going to the party?

Kate is having a birthday party. She sends invites to ten of her friends (Melissa, Evelyn, Emmy, Karen, Norma, Dorek, Agnes, Billy, Gaweł and Arthur).

Write a program that asks the user if each guest is attending. The program should store true or false for each person. The output from the program should be a list of names of everyone who is going to the party.

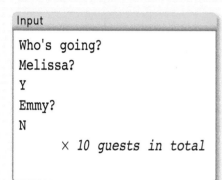

```
Input
Who's going?
Melissa?
Y
Emmy?
N
          × 10 guests in total
```

```
Output
Party Attendance List:
Melissa
Evelyn
Norma
Dorek
Billy
Gaweł
```

Program 53 – Bowling club day trip

Dunmore Bowling Club are organising a day out. Members are asked to choose a seat on the bus. The bus has five rows of seats with four seats on each row.

Write a program that first asks the user the enter the number of members that have requested to go on the trip. This should be limited to 20 members. The user should then enter each member's name and the row/seat number they have requested.

The program should assume that each member has asked for a different seat.

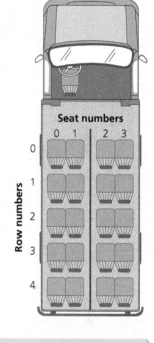

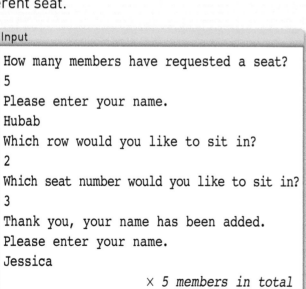

```
Input
How many members have requested a seat?
5
Please enter your name.
Hubab
Which row would you like to sit in?
2
Which seat number would you like to sit in?
3
Thank you, your name has been added.
Please enter your name.
Jessica
               × 5 members in total
```

```
Output
Bus seats have been booked as follows:
0. Empty Empty Empty Empty
1. Denzell Empty Hubub Empty
2. Jessica Empty Empty Empty
3. Empty Empty Talisha Empty
4. Empty Empty Empty Andrew
```

Program 54 – Counting weeds

A program is required to store the number of weeds found within a quadrat (5 by 5 grid of squares) that has been placed on a lawn.

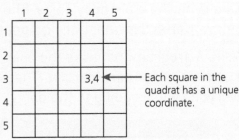

Each square in the quadrat has a unique coordinate.

The user should be asked to enter the number of weeds found at each coordinate (row and column), one at a time. When all the values have been entered the program should display the results as shown in the output below. The total number of weeds found, inside the quadrat area, should then be calculated and displayed.

Input

```
Please enter the number of weeds counted at 1,1: 3
Please enter the number of weeds counted at 1,2: 0
Please enter the number of weeds counted at 1,3: 2
Please enter the number of weeds counted at 1,4: 2
Please enter the number of weeds counted at 1,5: 0
Please enter the number of weeds counted at 2,1: 2

                            × 25 coordinates in total
```

Output

```
The results are shown below:
3 0 2 2 0
0 0 0 3 2
0 10 6 5 0
1 1 2 2 7
0 0 5 3 2
The total number of weeds found was - 56
```

Program 55 – Cricket over (part 3)

Southern District schools are organising a Speed Cricket tournament. Open and edit Program 48. The program needs to be edited to store 6 overs – 3 for each team – in a 2D list. It should calculate the score for each team and display the winner of the match. The program should then ask the user if they wish to calculate the result of another match. If the user selects "Y" the program should run again.

Input

```
Please enter over 1 for Team 1
2
1
0
0
6
6
Please enter over 2 for Team 1
0
                        × 3 overs in total for team 1
Please enter over 1 for Team 2
0
0
4
4
1
2
                        × 3 overs in total for team 2
Do you wish to calculate the result of another game?
Y
Please enter over 1 for Team 1
2
0
                               program repeats all inputs
```

Output

```
Score for Team 1's three overs:
27
Score for Team 2's three overs:
25
Team 1 won the match.
Do you wish to calculate the result of another game?
N
```

Section 5 – Predefined functions

All modern programming languages have predefined (built-in) functions that can be used by programmers to accomplish small tasks. These functions are pre-written bits of code that are "called" by your own programs when they are needed. The more functions you can learn, the greater the range of problems you can code and the easier it will be to code them.

In Section 1 you learned some simple functions to use with strings (len, count, upper, lower and replace) and some simple mathematical functions (round, int, modulus %, ceil and pow). One of the reasons that Python is such a fun programming language to learn is the large numbers of available functions built into the language. In this section we will learn and practise using some more complex predefined functions.

Chapter 20 – Examples of predefined functions

Example 43 – max( ) and min( )

The **max( )** and **min( )** functions allow the user to find the smallest or largest value in a list.

The two functions are **passed** a list within their brackets. This is called **parameter passing**.

Both functions return a value when they are used. If you wish to store the value for use later in your program you should store it in a variable. Alternatively, the returned value can just be displayed.

▼ Program Code

```
numbers = [12,4,67,55,29,2,89,23,99,6]
largest = max(numbers)
print ("The largest value is",largest)
print ("The smallest value is",min(numbers))
```

Output from program

```
The largest value is 99
The smallest value is 2
```

While the max( ) and min( ) functions would normally be used with numerical values (both integers and floats), they will also work with lists of strings. The minimum and maximum values will be the first and last alphabetically.

▼ Program Code

```
names = ["Bob","Aaliyah","Janet","Dave","Zac"]
print ("The largest value is",max(names))
print ("The smallest value is",min(names))
```

Output from program

```
The largest value is Zac
The smallest value is Aaliyah
```

Example 44 – sum( )

The **sum( )** function adds up numbers in a list and returns that value. It does not work for strings.

▼ Program Code

```
numbers = [12,4,67,55,29,2,89,23,99,6]
total = sum(numbers)
print ("The list total is",total)
```

Output from program [x]

```
The list total is 386
```

Example 45 – split( )

New lists can be created by splitting a string. The **split( )** function searches for a given character or string and splits the original string each time the search finds a match.

By searching for a space character " " a sentence can be split into its individual words with each word being stored separately in a new list. Note that, when found, the search character is removed from the string during the split.

▼ Program Code

```
sentence = "Demonstrate the split function."
words = [""]
words = sentence.split(" ")
for loop in range(len(words)):
        print(words[loop])
```

Output from program [x]

```
Demonstrate
the
split
function.
```

Any character or string can be used in the search. Note that the search string is still found if it is part of another word.

▼ Program Code

```
sentence = "Even if you're on the right
    track, you'll get run over if you just sit
    there."
words = [""]
words = sentence.split("you")
for loop in range(len(words)):
    print(words[loop])
```

Output from program [x]

```
Even if
're on the right track,
'll get run over if
 just sit there.
```

Example 46 – index( )

The **index( )** function finds the first position of a string or character within another string or list.

▼ Program Code

```
sentence = "Those who believe in telekinetics, raise my hand."
count = 0
count = sentence.index("w")
print(count)
```

Output from program ☒

```
6
```

The above program outputs the value 6 because the first character is index 0. If you remember back to the substring explanation near the beginning of the book each character's position can be defined as shown below.

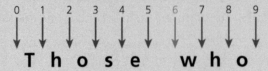

The index( ) function could be used with substring to split a string.

▼ Program Code

```
sentence = "It's time for the human race to enter the solar system."
firstHalf = ""
secondHalf = ""
firstHalf = sentence[ :sentence.index("to")]
secondHalf = sentence[sentence.index("to"): ]
print(firstHalf)
print(secondHalf)
```

Output from program ☒

```
It's time for the human race
to enter the solar system.
```

The index( ) function also works with numeric values and lists.

▼ Program Code

```
temperatures = [12.3,19.6,17.0,12.3,19.6]
idealTemp = 0
idealTemp = temperatures.index(19.6)
print("19.6 is stored at index",idealTemp)
```

Output from program ☒

```
19.6 is stored at index 1
```

Example 47 – Combining predefined functions

By combining two or more functions, programs can perform increasingly complicated, new tasks. The example below finds the position of the first occurrence of the maximum value in a list. Next it calculates the average of the values in a list using sum( ) and len( ). The code then uses these calculations to produce some meaningful information for the user.

▼ Program Code

```
milesCycled = [5,8,9,2,4,3,7,4,7,5,9,0]
bestDay = 0
average = 0
bestDay = milesCycled.index(max(milesCycled))
average = sum(milesCycled)/len(milesCycled)
print (max(milesCycled),"miles")
print ("were first cycled on day",bestDay+1)
print ("This was",max(milesCycled)-average)
print ("better than the average of",average)
```

Output from program ☒

```
9 miles
were cycled on day 3
This was 3.75
better than the average of 5.25
```

Example 48 – append( )

The append( ) function can only be used to add a single item to a list.

▼ Program Code

```
compUnits = ["byte","Kilobyte","Megabyte"]
compUnits.append("Gigabyte")
for each in compUnits:
    print(each)
```

Output from program ☒

```
byte
Kilobyte
Megabyte
Gigabyte
```

Note that a different style of fixed loop is used in this example. This line would read as: "for each item in the list compUnits". Each time the loop is executed the next item in the list is assigned to the loop variable 'each'.

append( ) is useful when creating a list of an unknown length. The programmer can initialise (create) a single element list and then each new value will simply be appended (added) onto the end of the list.

Example 49 – extend( )

To add more than one item to a list the **extend( )** function should be used. This effectively joins two lists together.

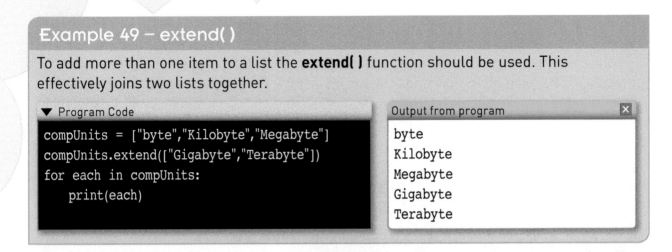

▼ Program Code

```
compUnits = ["byte","Kilobyte","Megabyte"]
compUnits.extend(["Gigabyte","Terabyte"])
for each in compUnits:
    print(each)
```

Output from program

```
byte
Kilobyte
Megabyte
Gigabyte
Terabyte
```

Example 50 – insert( )

The **insert( )** function is used to add new items at a specified index point in a list.

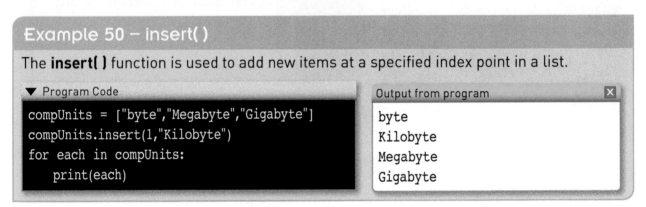

▼ Program Code

```
compUnits = ["byte","Megabyte","Gigabyte"]
compUnits.insert(1,"Kilobyte")
for each in compUnits:
    print(each)
```

Output from program

```
byte
Kilobyte
Megabyte
Gigabyte
```

In Example 50, "Kilobyte" replaces the item stored at index 1 in the list, which was until now "Megabyte".

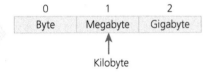

0	1	2
Byte	Megabyte	Gigabyte

↑
Kilobyte

Megabyte and Gigabyte move one place in the list, becoming indexes 2 and 3.

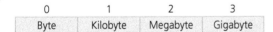

0	1	2	3
Byte	Kilobyte	Megabyte	Gigabyte

Example 51 – pop( )

Items can be removed from a list using **pop( )** and **remove( )**.

The pop( ) function removes an item according to its index value. So pop(0) would remove the first value from the list.

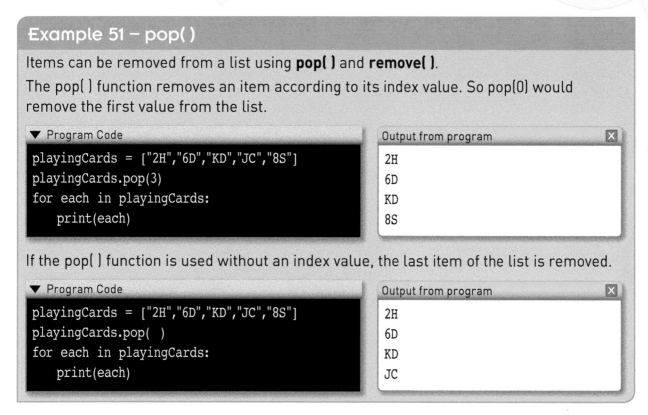

▼ Program Code
```
playingCards = ["2H","6D","KD","JC","8S"]
playingCards.pop(3)
for each in playingCards:
    print(each)
```

Output from program
```
2H
6D
KD
8S
```

If the pop( ) function is used without an index value, the last item of the list is removed.

▼ Program Code
```
playingCards = ["2H","6D","KD","JC","8S"]
playingCards.pop( )
for each in playingCards:
    print(each)
```

Output from program
```
2H
6D
KD
JC
```

Example 52 – remove( )

The remove( ) function removes the first example of a named item from a list.

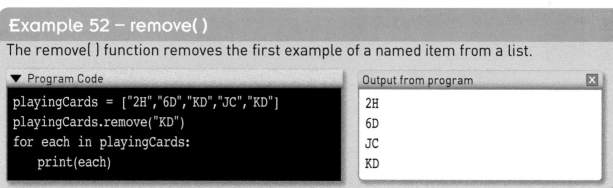

▼ Program Code
```
playingCards = ["2H","6D","KD","JC","KD"]
playingCards.remove("KD")
for each in playingCards:
    print(each)
```

Output from program
```
2H
6D
JC
KD
```

Example 53 – random.randint( )

The **randint( )**, or random integer function, generates a random integer within a stated range.

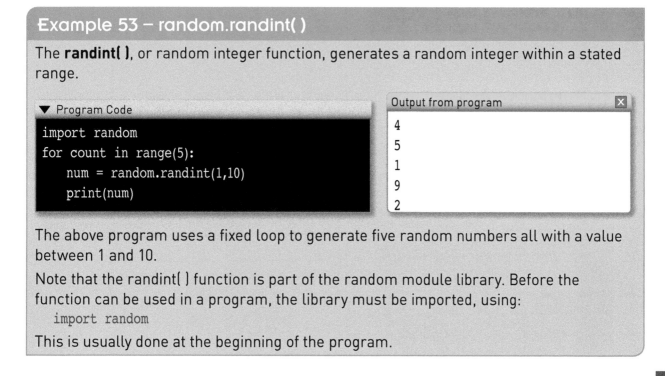

Output from program
```
4
5
1
9
2
```

▼ Program Code
```
import random
for count in range(5):
    num = random.randint(1,10)
    print(num)
```

The above program uses a fixed loop to generate five random numbers all with a value between 1 and 10.

Note that the randint( ) function is part of the random module library. Before the function can be used in a program, the library must be imported, using:
```
import random
```
This is usually done at the beginning of the program.

Chapter 21 – Computational thinking puzzles (predefined functions)

These puzzles are all about following the output from each function.

Puzzle set 12 – Predefined functions (max, min, sum, split, index, append)

The first puzzles will use single functions and should be relatively easy.

120
```
hoursStudied = [2,4,6,3,4,2,3,4,2,3,1]
print("The most hours studied in")
print("a day was",max(hoursStudied))
```
Output

121
```
hoursPlayed = [7,3,4,5,2,3,4,8,2,9,10]
print("The least hours played in")
print("a day was",min(hoursPlayed))
```
Output

122
```
weight = [12,8,3,7,14,6]
totalWeight = sum(weight)
print("The total weight is:",totalWeight)
```
Output

123
```
numList = [3,8,30,72,3,7,7,23,41,99,2,1,8,92]
limits = [ ]
limits.append(min(numList))
limits.append(max(numList))
manPlusMax = sum(limits)
print("Minimum",limits[0],"+ Maximum",limits[1],"=",manPlusMax)
```
Output

124
```
numList = [3,8,30,72,3,7,7,23,41,99,2,1,8,92]
limits = [ ]
limits.append(numList[0])
limits.append(numList[3])
limits.append(numList[6])
limits.append(numList[7])
limits.append(numList[10])
print("Maximum =",max(limits))
print("Minimum =",min(limits))
```
Output

125
```
shoppingList = "Peas,Carrots,Milk,Tea Bags,Bread,Marmalade"
shopping = shoppingList.split(",")
for each in shopping:
    print(each)
```
Output

126
```
cricketScores = "2,3,0,0,0,1-0,0,0,2,3,0-1,1,0,0,0,6"
overScores = cricketScores.split("-")
for loop in range(len(overScores)):
    oneOver = overScores[loop]
    print("The first ball =",oneOver[0:1])
```
Output

127
```
pageLength = "123 949 823 546 1002 398"
eachBookLength = pageLength.split(" ")
longestBook = max(eachBookLength)
print("The longest book =",longestBook, "pages. ")
```
Output

128
```
pageLength = "123 949 823 546 1002 398"
eachBookLength = pageLength.split(" ")
for loop in range(len(eachBookLength)):
    eachBookLength[loop] = int(eachBookLength[loop])
longestBook = max(eachBookLength)
print("The longest book =",longestBook,"pages.")
```
Output

129
```
allTemperatures = "12,11,10,4,-2,5,8,20,23,24"
temperatures = allTemperatures.split(",")
for loop in range(len(temperatures)):
    temperatures[loop] = int(temperatures[loop])
print("The lowest temp =",min(temperatures))
print("The highest temp =",max(temperatures))
```
Output

130
```
lyric = "If love's so easy, why's it hard?"
letterPosition = lyric.index("o")
print("The letter is at position",letterPosition)
```
Output

131
```
vocals = ["say","speak","dictate","verbalise","shout"]
wordPosition = vocals.index("shout")
print("The word is at position",wordPosition)
```
Output

132
```
sentence = "Here's looking at you, kid."
words = sentence.split(" ")
wordPosition = words.index("at")
print("The word is at position",wordPosition)
```
Output

Puzzle set 13 – Predefined functions (pop, insert, remove, extend and append)

These next puzzles are like the card trick where you are shown three cards, you choose one and they are then swapped around and you have to guess where your chosen card is.

Keep an eye on how each function changes the list. You may find it useful to make notes on paper to help you.

For each puzzle, state what will be displayed at the end when the program is executed.

133
```
light = [2,4,6,8,10]
light.pop(2)
light.append(7)
print(light)
```
Output

134
```
light = [1,3,5,7,11]
light.pop(3)
light.pop(3)
light.remove(1)
print(light)
```
Output

135
```
light = [3,4,5,6]
light.insert(0,2)
light.pop(2)
light.append(1)
print(light)
```
Output

136
```
light = [44,33,66,44,55,44]
for loop in range(3):
    light.remove(44)
print(light)
```
Output

137
```
days = [4,6,4,5,8,2,4]
nights = []
temp = days.pop(2)
nights.append(temp)
nights.append(temp+1)
nights.append(temp+2)
print(nights)
```
Output

138
```
sequence = [1,2,3,4,5]
for loop in range(4):
    temp = sequence.pop(0)
    sequence.append(temp)
print(sequence)
```
Output

139
```
days = [4,6,4,5,8,2,4]
nights = []
for loop in range(5,0,-1):
    temp = days.pop(loop)
    nights.append(temp + loop)
print(nights)
```
Output

140
```
light = [5,1,3,1,4]
for loop in range(3):
    if light[loop] > 1:
        light.remove(light[loop])
print(light)
```
Output

141
```
points = [3,4,5,1,3,1,4]
above = []
average = sum(points)/len(points)
for loop in range(len(points)):
    if points[loop] > average:
        above.append(points[loop])
print(above)
```
Output

142 And finally a very difficult one. State what is stored and displayed in list "three".

```
one = [3,4,5,1,5,1,4,3]
two = []
three = []
for loop in range(len(one)-1,-1,-1):
    two.append(one[loop])
for loop in range(len(one)):
    if one[loop]==two[loop]:
        three.append(1)
    else:
        three.append(0)
print(three)
```

Output

Chapter 22 – Programming challenges for Section 5

The following program challenges will all involve working with lists and functions.

The syntax covered in Section 5 was:

Predefined Functions	Examples
• max( )	• max(nameList)
• min( )	• min(speedLists)
• sum( )	• sum(heights)
• split( )	• sentence.split("a")
• index( )	• phrase.index("as")
• append( )	• names.append("George")
• extend( )	• members.extend(newMembers)
• insert( )	• names.insert(3,"Yusuf")
• pop( )	• times.pop(3)
• remove( )	• times.remove(12.45)
• random.randint( )	• random.randint(20,40)

By this stage the programs you are writing should be getting longer and more complex. Using the functions in short pieces of code is relatively easy, so these challenges will focus on more complex scenarios. Decide what functions you will need and how you will use them to solve the challenges.

Program challenges for predefined functions

Program 56 – Guess the number (part 2)

Using the random integer function, open and edit Program 43 to make the program randomly generate the number (from 1 to 100) that the user is asked to guess. The program should run as before, so the inputs and outputs should not change.

Program 57 – Comic collector

Anita has given her collection of Super Rat comic books to her friend Liam. Liam currently owns issues 1, 2, 3, 7, 8, 9, 10 and 16 of the comic. Write a program that will store the issues already owned by Liam and then ask the user to enter a single input of the issue numbers Anita is donating. The program should create a new list from the input. The new list should then be added to Liam's currently owned comic list. The final combined list should be displayed.

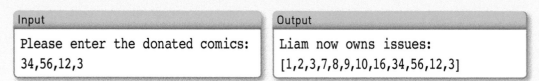

```
Input
Please enter the donated comics:
34,56,12,3
```

```
Output
Liam now owns issues:
[1,2,3,7,8,9,10,16,34,56,12,3]
```

Program 58 – Dress sizes

A program is required to store information on all the dress sizes currently stocked in a charity shop. As new dresses are donated, the size of the dress should be stored in a list. The up-to-date list is then displayed. If a customer buys a dress, one value of that size should be removed from the list. If the user enters 999 as the size of a donated dress, the program should display the largest and smallest dress sizes in stock.

```
Input
Do you wish to add (A) or remove (R) a dress?
A
Please enter a new dress size: 12
Stock = [12]
Do you wish to add (A) or remove (R) a dress?
A
Please enter a new dress size: 14
Stock = [12,14]
Do you wish to add (A) or remove (R) a dress?
R
Please enter a new dress size: 12
Stock = [14]
Do you wish to add (A) or remove (R) as dress?
A
                    × several more dress sizes
Please enter a new dress size: 999
```

```
Output
Stock = [12,10,8,10,12,14,16,20,12,12,8]
The largest dress in stock is size 20
The smallest dress in stock is size 8
```

Program 59 – Which is bigger?

Write a program that generates two random integers between 1 and 1000. A user is asked to guess which of the two numbers is the largest. If they guess correctly, they score a point. The program should repeat this process ten times and then display the player's total points.

```
Input
I have generated two random numbers.
Which is the largest, 1 or 2?
Enter your choice.
1
     × 10 pairs of numbers and guesses
```

```
Output
Number 1 = 459
Number 2 = 321
Correct, number 1 was the largest.
               × 10 pairs of numbers and results
Your total was 6 correct guesses out of 10
Your final score was 6 correct.
```

Program 60 – Meal vouchers

Members of a small theatre group decide that, after their Saturday show, they will treat their oldest audience member to vouchers for an Italian meal. As each audience member arrives for the chosen show, they are asked their age and the seat number they are sitting in. A program is required to store the audience's ages and seat numbers (between 1 and 56) as they arrive at the theatre. If the audience member would prefer not to give their age it should be stored as 0. The code should find and display the seat number of the oldest audience member. If two audience members are the same age, the vouchers should be awarded to the one who arrived first.

The manager of the theatre also wishes to know how many of the customers refused to give their age.

```
Input

Enter age: 45
Enter seat: 27
Do you wish to enter another: Y
Enter age: 89
Enter seat: 4
Do you wish to enter another: Y
          × audience members until N is entered
Enter age: 0
Enter seat: 49
Do you wish to enter another: N
```

```
Output

The oldest audience member is sitting in seat 4
6 audience members did not give their age.
```

Program 61 – Diving scores

Diving events are scored by a panel of seven judges, who each score a dive between 0 and 10. Of the seven scores, the top two and the bottom two are discarded. The remaining three scores are added together and multiplied by the dive's difficulty rating. Write a program that will accept seven judges' scores, entered as a single string, and the dive's difficulty. The diver's calculated score should be displayed.

```
Input

Please enter the judges' scores:
7,8,6,9,6,8,4
Please enter the difficulty rating:
3.4
```

```
Output

The three remaining judges' scores are:
7
6
8
The diver's score is: 71.4
```

Program 62 – Dice solitaire game

A dice game has the following rules:

- The player rolls one six-sided dice.
- If the player rolls a number that isn't written down already, they write it down on the paper.
- If the player rolls a number that is already written down, the number should be crossed out and the player loses that number.
- The player repeats the above until every number (1, 2, 3, 4, 5 and 6) is written down.

Write a program that will play the game and display how many rolls it took to complete the game. The program should generate a random number between 1 and 6 to simulate each dice roll. The code will have to check if each random number is already in the list before adding or removing the dice roll. The program should keep looping until the list is six elements long.

```
Output
Dice rolled = 3
After roll 1: [3]
Dice rolled = 2
After roll 2: [3,2]
Dice rolled = 4
After roll 3: [3,2,4]
Dice rolled = 3
After roll 4: [2,4]
                × several more dice rolls
Dice rolled = 1
After roll 25: [3,6,4,2,5,1]
Game completed in 25 rolls of the dice.
```

Section 6 – Modular programming

When learning to write code, everyone begins by writing **sequential programs**. Despite looping occasionally or branching (if), sequential programs essentially run from the first line to the last. In reality no professional program is written that way.

Professional programmers like to reuse code that they have previously written. This saves time when developing new programs. If part of their program performs a complex calculation or task, programmers will separate that code out and write it in a separate block or **module**. This is called **modular programming**. Modules are then **called** by the main part of the program when they are required to carry out their calculation or task.

An example of a sequential and modular version of the same program is shown below. The highlighted code performs the task of displaying "nameList". In the modular version these lines have been lifted out of the main program and placed inside a module.

Program code (sequential)

```python
nameList = [["Matthew","Reid"]]
numNames = int(input("How many names do you wish to add?"))
for names in range(numNames):
  newForename = str(input("Please enter a forename"))
  newSurname = str(input("Please enter a surname"))
  nameList.append([newForename,newSurname])
  print("Current list:")
for loop in range(len(nameList)):
  print("Forename",nameList[loop][0])
  print("Surname",nameList[loop][1])
```

The highlighted code performs the task of displaying "nameList". In the modular version these lines have been lifted out of the main program and placed inside a module.

Program code (modular)

```python
def displayNames(nameList):
  print(""Current list:")
  for loop in range(len(nameList)):
    print("Forename",nameList[loop][0])
    print("Surname",nameList[loop][1])

nameList = [["Matthew","Reid"]]
numNames = int(input("How many names do you wish to add?"))
for names in range(numNames):
  newForename = str(input("Please enter a forename"))
  newSurname = str(input("Please enter a surname"))
  nameList.append([newForename,newSurname])
displayNames(nameList)
```

Chapter 23 – Examples of modular programming

There are two common types of module used in programming:

- **Procedure** – A block of code that performs a process
- **Function** – A block of code that performs a process (often a calculation) and then returns the result of that process to the main program.

In Python, both of these types of module use the same **def( )** or **definition statement**.

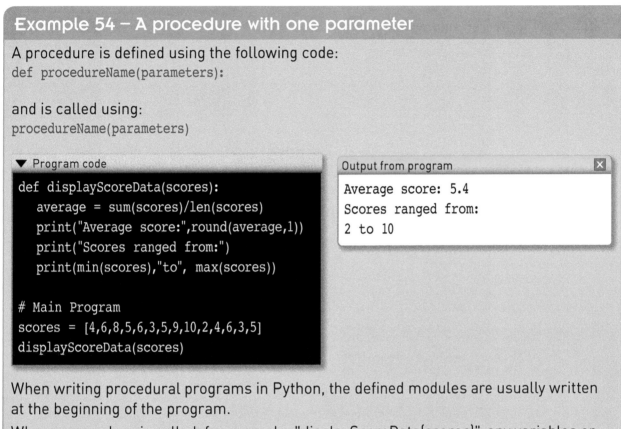

Example 54 – A procedure with one parameter

A procedure is defined using the following code:
```
def procedureName(parameters):
```

and is called using:
```
procedureName(parameters)
```

▼ Program code
```
def displayScoreData(scores):
    average = sum(scores)/len(scores)
    print("Average score:",round(average,1))
    print("Scores ranged from:")
    print(min(scores),"to", max(scores))


# Main Program
scores = [4,6,8,5,6,3,5,9,10,2,4,6,3,5]
displayScoreData(scores)
```

Output from program ☒
```
Average score: 5.4
Scores ranged from:
2 to 10
```

When writing procedural programs in Python, the defined modules are usually written at the beginning of the program.

When a procedure is called, for example, "displayScoreData(scores)", any variables or lists that will be used by the module are passed as parameters. Parameters are placed within the brackets of the call statement and the brackets of the def( ) statement.

Example 55 – A procedure with multiple parameters

It is common to pass more than one variable or list into a procedure.

▼ Program code

```python
def displayWinner(player1,player2):
    player1Wins = 0
    player2Wins = 0
    draws = 0
    for loop in range(len(player1)):
        if player1[loop]>player2[loop]:
            player1Wins = player1Wins + 1
        if player2[loop]>player1[loop]:
            player2Wins = player2Wins + 1
        if player2[loop]==player1[loop]:
            draws = draws + 1
    print("Player 1 has",player1Wins,"wins.")
    print("Player 2 has",player2Wins,"wins.")
    print("There were",draws,"draws.")


# Main Program
player1 = [4,6,8,5,6]
player2 = [2,9,8,5,3]
displayWinner(player1,player2)
```

Output from program ☒

```
Player 1 has 2 wins.
Player 2 has 1 wins.
There were 2 draws.
```

Example 56 – Writing to reuse code

The following example shows how a procedure can be written in a way that allows its reuse in different scenarios.

▼ Program code

```
def displayData(dataInput,message):
    average = sum(dataInput)/len(dataInput)
    print("Average " + message.lower(),round(average,1))
    print(message + "s ranged from:")
    print(min(dataInput),"to", max(dataInput))
    print()


# Main Program
scores = [4,6,8,5,6,3,5,9,10,2,4,6,3,5]
title = "Score"
displayData(scores,title)

phReadings = [3.4,3.7,3.0,4.2,5.0,2.7,3.2]
text = "pH"
displayData(pHReadings,text)

heights = [154,158,187,172,155,190,182]
word = "Height"
displayData(heights,word)
```

Output from program ☒

```
Average score 5.4
Scores ranged from:
2 to 10

Average pH 3.6
pHs ranged from:
2.7 to 5.0

Average height 171.1
Heights ranged from:
154 to 190
```

The parameters in the procedure definition are different from the parameters in the call from the main program. This is useful when we wish to use a module with different variables and lists.

- The parameters in the procedure call are called "**actual**" parameters.
- The parameters in the procedure definition are called "**formal**" parameters.

When a procedure or function is called, the actual parameters are copied into the formal parameters.

Example 57 – A function returning a value

There are two differences between a function and a procedure in Python.

After a defined function carries out its task or calculation, it "returns" the result.

When a function returns this result it must be stored somewhere, so the result is usually **assigned**. This means a **function call** looks slightly different from a **procedure call**:

- procedure call: `calculateArea(length, width)`
- function call: `area = calculateArea(length, width)`.

▼ Program code

```
def interestCalculator(loan,period,interest):
    total = loan
    for years in range(period):
        total = total * (1+interest/100)
    return total


# Main Program
amount = int(input("Enter borrowing amount"))
years = int(input("Enter length of loan (years)"))
interest = float(input("Enter rate of interest"))
repayment = interestCalculator(amount,years,interest)
print("Repayment amount =", round(repayment, 2))
```

Output from program ☒

```
Repayment amount = 1331.0
```

The above output was generated by inputting:

1000

3

10

It is possible to use the result returned from a function without assigning it. For example, the last two lines of the example program could be written in one line of code:

```
print("Repayment amount =", round(interestCalculator(amount,years,interest),2))
```

Example 58 – Scope

The following program displays the average, calculated in the procedure, in two different places:

1 within the procedure

2 within the main program.

▼ Program code

```
def displayScoreData(scores):
    average = sum(scores)/len(scores)
    print("Average score:",round(average,1))
    print("Scores ranged from:")
    print(min(scores),"to", max(scores))


# Main Program
average = 0
scores = [4,6,8,5,6,3,5,9,10,2,4,6,3,5]
displayScoreData(scores)
print()
print("Average score:",round(average,1))
```

Output from program   ☒

```
Average score: 5.4
Scores ranged from:
2 to 10

Average score: 0
```

When this program executes, a list, "scores", is passed into the procedure where the (mean) average of the values in the list is calculated and displayed. At the bottom of the main program (after the procedure has been called and the average calculated) the average is displayed again.

While you would expect that the same average (5.4) would be displayed twice, the average displayed in the main program is 0.

This anomaly occurs because any variable or list that is initialised (created) within a procedure only exists within that procedure. The **scope** of the "average" variable within the procedure is said to be **local**.

The "average" variable initialised in the main program is said to have **global** scope as it can be used anywhere in the main program.

Good coding separates out as many reusable blocks of code as possible. The purpose of parameter passing is to share the data between modules and the main program. Functions return values as this allows the results of the calculation or task to exist outside the function.

Chapter 24 – Computational thinking puzzles (modular programming)

These puzzles have been created to practise your understanding of modular programming including:

- parameter passing
- procedures
- functions
- local
- global

Puzzle set 14 – Modular programming

The code in the puzzles below calls the following procedure and functions.

```
def module1(first,second,third):
    volume = first * second * third
    print("Volume =",volume)
def module2(monday):
    monday = monday/10
    return monday
def module3(blue,red):
    total = 0
    for counter in range(blue,red):
        total = total + 2
    print(total)
    return total
def module4(up,down):
    middle = up%down
    top = int(up/down)
    total = middle + top
    return total
```

For each of the following puzzles write down the output that would be displayed.

143
```
num1 = 2
num2 = 3
num3 = 4
module1(num1,num2,num3)
```
Output

144
```
num1 = 8
num2 = 3
value = module4(num1,num2)
print(value)
```
Output

145
```
num1 = 100
num2 = 6
num3 = 9
print(module2(num1) + module3(num2,num3))
```
Output

146
```
num1 = 5
num2 = 10
temp = int(module2(num2))
value = module3(temp,num1)
print(value)
```

Output

147
```
num1 = 2
num2 = 5
num3 = 8
module1(num1,module3(num1,num2),module2(5*num3))
```

Output

Puzzles 148 to 155 contain code that calls the following functions. The functions return different values depending on the parameters passed in.

```
def textChanger1(word):
    wordLength = len(word)
    if wordLength <=2:
        return word
    elif wordLength>2 and wordLength<=6:
        temp1 = word[0:2]
        temp2 = word[len(word)-2:]
        word = temp2 + word + temp1
        return word
    else:
        temp1 = word[0:3]
        temp2 = word[len(word)-3:]
        print(temp1,temp2)
        word = temp2 + temp1
        return word
def textChanger2(word):
    if word.lower() == word:
        return word.upper()
    elif word.upper() == word:
        return word.lower()
    else:
        return "mixed"
def textChanger3(word):
    length = 5 * len(word)
    word = str(length-5) + word + str(length)
    return word
```

For each of the following puzzles write down the output that would be displayed.

148
```
password = "voted"
password = textChanger1(password)
print("Password is",password)
```

Output

149
```
password = "LOADED"
password = textChanger2(password)
print("Password is",password)
```

Output

150
```
password = "Hidden"
password = textChanger3(password)
print("Password is",password)
```

Output

151
```
password = "Dug"
password = textChanger2(password)
password = textChanger3(password)
print("Password is",password)
```

Output

152
```
password = "xu"
password = textChanger3(password)
password = textChanger2(password)
password = textChanger1(password)
print("Password is",password)
```

Output

153
```
password = "gnome"
password = textChanger3(password)
password = textChanger2(password)
password = textChanger1(password)
print("Password is",password)
```

Output

154
```
password = "Bruv"
password = textChanger2(password)
password = textChanger2(password)
password = textChanger3(password)
password = textChanger3(password)
print("Password is",password)
```

Output

155
```
password = "hard"
password = textChanger3
(textChanger2(textChanger1(password))) print("Password is",password)
```

Output

Chapter 25 – Programming challenges for Section 6

The syntax covered in Section 6 was:

Statements and syntax	Examples
• def( )	• def calculateArea(length,width):
	• calculateArea(length,width)

While some of these challenges are new, several require that you rewrite challenges from earlier sections. This restructuring of programs is a useful way of reinforcing how modular programming works without having to do a great deal of problem solving at the same time.

Once you have developed the skill of modular programming, you should ensure that every program you write in the future is developed using that style of programming.

Program challenges for modular programming

Program 63 – Dress sizes (part 2)

Open Program 58. Edit the program as follows:

- After the user has entered 999, tell the user that they can find out how many items of one dress size are in stock if they enter another dress size.
- Pass the dress size list and the above user-inputted dress size to a new function.
- The function should count the number of dresses in the list that match the size given by the user.
- The number of matching dresses found should be returned from the function.
- The main program should display the result with a suitable message.

```
Input
                 previous inputs as before
Please enter a new dress size: 999
Enter a dress size to count:   12
```

```
Output
There are 4 size 12 dresses in stock
Stock = [12,10,8,10,12,14,16,20,12,12,8]
The largest dress in stock is size 20
The smallest dress in stock is size 8
```

Program 64 – Charity collection (part 5)

Open Program 34. Edit the program as follows:

- The number of charity raisers entered by the user should be passed to a function. The function should calculate and return the total money raised.
- A procedure should be created to make the decision about the final amount raised (see Program 27) and display any appropriate messages.

Note that the inputs and outputs from the program should not change.

Program 65 – Cycling speed (part 2)

Open Program 19. Edit the program as follows:

- Rather than asking for the details of one journey (using wheel revolutions and minutes taken), the program should ask the user to enter the number of journeys they have completed.

- A loop should be used to ask for the wheel revolutions and minutes for each of these journeys. The values entered should be stored using two lists.

- A function then needs to be coded to
  - calculate the total distance covered in km
  - return the total distance where it can be displayed in the main program.

- A second function then needs to be written to
  - calculate the total number of minutes cycled over all the journeys
  - calculate the average speed over all the journeys in km per hour
  - return the average speed to the main program where it can be displayed in a message.

To successfully complete this program, you will have to work out what must be passed into the two functions.

```
Input
What is the circumference of your wheel in millimetres?
1250
How many journeys do you wish to enter?
3
Journey 1
How many wheel revolutions have taken place in your journey?
8920
How many minutes did you cycle for?
30
Journey 2
How many wheel revolutions have taken place in your journey?
10299
How many minutes did you cycle for?
40
Journey 3
How many wheel revolutions have taken place in your journey?
4920
How many minutes did you cycle for?
26
```

```
Output
You covered 30.17 km.
At an average speed of 18.9 kmph.
```

Program 66 – Counting weeds (part 2)

Open Program 54. The program should be edited as follows:

- After all weeds are entered, pass the 2D list, as a parameter, to a new function.
- The function should count the total number of weeds stored in the 2D list.
- The total number of weeds should be returned from the function.
- The total number of weeds should then be passed to a new procedure.
- The procedure should display different messages based on the number of weeds:
  - < 2: "You have a great, well looked after lawn."
  - >= 2 and <= 10: "A bit of light weeding will help your lawn look great."
  - >10 and <50: "Your lawn should be treated with an environmentally friendly weed killer."
  - >= 50: "We would advise that your lawn is dug up and re-laid."

```
Output (using previous input from program 54)
The results are shown below:
3 0 2 2 0
0 0 0 3 2
0 10 6 5 0
1 1 2 2 7
0 0 5 3 2
The total number of weeds found was – 56
We would advise that your lawn is dug up and re-laid.
```

Program 67 – Password generator

Using puzzles 148 to 155 as a starting point, develop your own modular password generator program. The program should:

- contain at least four text scrambling functions (two can be functions used in the puzzles)
- ask the user to enter a word
- generate a random number from 1 to 3
- call different combinations of the text scrambling functions for each possible random number (1, 2 or 3).

After the text has been scrambled, the program should:

- ensure that the final password is exactly ten characters long
- display the password.

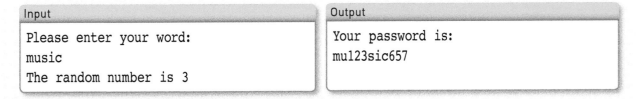

```
Input
Please enter your word:
music
The random number is 3
```

```
Output
Your password is:
mu123sic657
```

Section 7 – File handling

You may have noticed that each time you run your programs you have to re-enter every input. This is, of course, unrealistic. The majority of programs store information while the code is not running. For example:

- A console game will store your progress through the game along with game credits, in-game purchases, results of previous games and even video replays saved by the user.
- A banking app on a phone will access your account details and call up spending and deposits in your account.
- A social media website will store your posts, pictures you've uploaded, your likes and your replies to other users' posts.

In all of the above scenarios, the data will either be stored in an external file or in a database. Data will be read from the file/database into the program when it is needed. When new data is stored we say it will be written to the file/database.

The following section will explain how Python can be used to read from and write to .txt and .csv files.

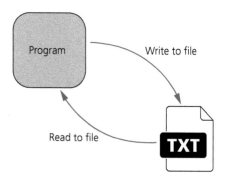

Figure 25.1: Read/write to file.

Note: If you wish to research reading and writing from databases, you will need to install Python's MySQL Connector library. Instructions on how to set this up and connect to/communicate with a database file are available online. Later versions of Python may have SQLite built into the installation so check your version first.

Chapter 26 – Examples of file handling

The open( ) statement is used to connect to an external (saved) file. For example:

```
with open('test.txt','r') as fileConn
```

Two parameters are passed by the open statement:

- 'text.txt' – the first parameter is the name of file. For all the examples in this book the external file should be located in the same folder as the saved Python program.
- 'r' – the second parameter is the type of connection that will be made to the file.

The types of connections that can be made are as follows:

- 'r' when information is only read from the file
- 'w' when information is only written to a file; this overwrites any information that was already stored in the file
- 'a' to append (write) information to the end of a file, without overwriting what is already stored
- 'r+' to read and write to the same file.

Each connection is assigned to a variable, in this case "fileConn". This is so that connections could be opened to multiple files:

```
with open('jan.txt','r') as janConn
with open('feb.txt','r') as febConn
with open('mar.txt','w') as marConn
```

Example 59 – Writing to a text file

Python is able to connect to an existing text file or to create a text file if it does not exist.

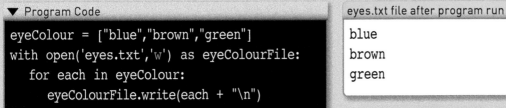

▼ Program Code

```
eyeColour = ["blue","brown","green"]
with open('eyes.txt','w') as eyeColourFile:
    for each in eyeColour:
        eyeColourFile.write(each + "\n")
```

eyes.txt file after program run

```
blue
brown
green
```

The above program opens a **write only connection** "w" to a text file called "eyes.txt".

A loop is then used to write each element of a list to the file using the connection "eyeColourFile" and the function **write( )**.

Note that the string "\n" is concatenated onto the end of each line. This is an "end-of-line" character. When a text file is opened the \n character ensures that the next item of text appears on a new line.

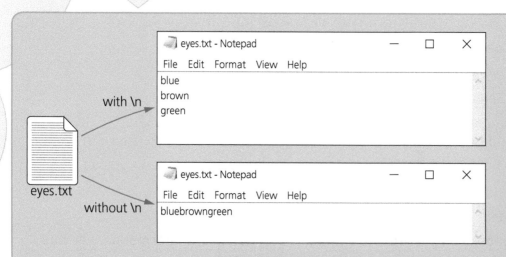

If the text file does not exist when a write only connection is attempted, an empty file will be created.

The connection to the file is closed at the end of the with open( ) statement.

Note that even if this program were executed lots of times, the file would still store the colours. The "w" connection type means that the previous information is overwritten each time the program is executed.

Example 60 – Appending a text file

Rather than overwriting the information stored in a file, we may wish to simply add more to it.

▼ Program Code

```
hairColour = ["brown","red","white","black","blonde"]
with open('eyes.txt','a') as hairColourFile:
    for each in hairColour:
        hairColourFile.write(each+"\n")
```

eyes.txt file after program run ☒

```
blue
brown
green
brown
red
white
black
blonde
```

The above program opens an **append connection** "a" to the file "eyes.txt" used in Example 60. As before, a loop is used to write all the items of a list to the file. This time the list items are appended to the end of the file.

Example 61 – Reading from a text file into separate lists

Reading from a text file involves a three-stage process:

- Open a connection (**read only** or **read/write**).
- Read all the lines from the file using the **readlines( )** function.
- Store the information in each line.

The code for each of these bullet points has been highlighted in the example program below.

While the first two bullets are easy, the last one often requires a bit more thought.

For example, Matthew has a text file which stores the name of the friends he's planning a holiday with. Each line of the text file is formatted as follows:

Matthew Reid Schmeed/n

To store each friend's forename, surname and nickname in three lists called "forename", "surname" and "nickname" we would have to:

1 remove the end-of-line characters (/n) using substring – [0:-1]

2 split each line (which is stored as a string) using the split( ) function

3 allocate each element of the list created by the split( ) function to one of the three lists.

▼ Program Code

```
forename = []
surname = []
nickname = []
with open('Friends.txt','r') as pals:

    for each in pals.readlines():

        each = each[0:-1]                    (1)

        temp = each.split(" ")               (2)
        forename.append(temp[0])
        surname.append(temp[1])              (3)
        nickname.append(temp[2])

print(forename)
print(surname)
print(nickname)
```

Original text file

```
Matthew Reid Schmeed/n
Niall Dowds Jas/n
Emir Duman Meter/n
Lewis Carter Momo/n
Steven Moyles Beve/n
```

Output from program

```
['Matthew','Niall','Emir','Lewis','Steven']
['Reid','Dowds','Duman','Carter','Moyles']
['Schmeed','Jas','Meter','Momo','Beve']
```

Note that each line has been split using a space character as there is a space between each word in the file. This can be replaced with a comma where the file information is comma separated as with .csv files.

Program Code

```
forename = []
surname = []
nickname = []
with open('Friends.csv','r') as pals:
    for each in pals.readlines():
        each = each[0:-1]
        temp = each.split(",")
        forename.append(temp[0])
        surname.append(temp[1])
        nickname.append(temp[2])
print(forename)
print(surname)
print(nickname)
```

Original text file

```
Matthew,Reid,Schmeed/n
Niall,Dowds,Jas/n
Emir,Duman,Meter/n
Lewis,Carter,Momo/n
Steven,Moyles,Beve/n
```

Output from program

```
['Matthew','Niall','Emir','Lewis','Steven']
['Reid','Dowds','Duman','Carter','Moyles']
['Schmeed','Jas','Meter','Momo','Beve']
```

Example 62 – Reading from a text file into a 2D list

Using the same scenario as the previous example, we can see that reading the same text file and storing the information in a 2D list is actually easier and requires fewer lines of code.

Program Code

```
names = []
with open('Friends.txt','r') as pals:
    for each in pals.readlines():
        each = each[0:-1]
        temp = each.split(" ")
        names.append(temp)
print(names)
```

Original text file

```
Matthew Reid Schmeed
Niall Dowds Jas
Emir Duman Meter
Lewis Carter Momo
Steven Moyles Beve
```

Output from program

```
[['Matthew','Reid','Schmeed'], ['Niall',
'Dowds','Jas'], ['Emir','Duman','Meter'],
['Lewis','Carter','Momo'], ['Steven',
'Moyles','Beve']]
```

Using the split( ) function on each line creates the sublist of the 2D list so all that remains to do is create a new element of the main list by appending each sublist.

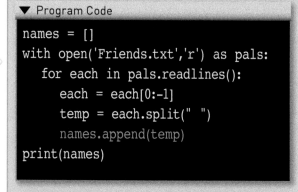

names	second index		
first index	0	1	2
0	Matthew	Reid	Schmeed
1	Niall	Dowds	Jas
2	Emir	Duman	Meter
3	Lewis	Carter	Momo
4	Steven	Moyles	Beve

Chapter 27 – Computational thinking puzzles (file handling)

The following puzzles are designed to improve your understanding of how files are read from and written to. Follow the code carefully and see if you can predict the output produced by either print( ) or write( ).

Puzzle set 15 – File handling

For each puzzle below write down the text that would be stored in the file.

156
```
bikes = ["Perseid","Lomond","Retford","Timbuktu"]
count = 1
with open('bikes.txt','w') as bikeFile:
    for each in bikes:
        bikeFile.write(str(count) + ". " + each + "\n")
        count = count + 1
```

Output

157
```
sizes = ["12","23","16","08"]
moreSizes = ["10","20",]
with open('sizes.txt','w') as sizeFile:
    for each in moreSizes:
        sizeFile.write(str(each)+"\n")
with open('sizes.txt','a') as sizeFile:
    for each in sizes:
        sizeFile.write(str(each)+"\n")
```

Output

158
```
keys = ["q","w","e","r"]
keysTwo = ["a","s","d","f"]
with open('keyboard.txt','w') as keysFile:
    for each in keys:
        keysFile.write(each)
with open('keyboard.txt','w') as keysFile:
    for each in keysTwo:
        keysFile.write(each)
```

Output

159 The file "elements.txt" is shown below.

```
elements.txt
Oxygen
Neon
Mercury
```

State the output from the following program.

```
elements = []
with open('elements.txt','r') as elem:
    for each in elem.readlines():
        print(each[0:-1])
```

Output

160 The file "presidents.txt" is shown below.

```
presidents.txt

George Washington
John Adams
Thomas Jefferson
James Madison
```

State the output from the following program.

```
presidents = []
with open('presidents.txt','r') as pres:
    for each in pres.readlines():
        each = each[0:-1]
        presidents.append(each)
for loop in range(len(presidents)):
    print(presidents[loop])
```

161 Using the same presidents.txt file, state the output from the following program.

```
presidents = ["James Monroe","John Quincy Adams"]
with open('presidents.txt','r') as pres:
    for each in pres.readlines():
        presidents.append(each[0:-1])
for loop in range(len(presidents)):
    print(str(loop+1)+". "+presidents[loop])
```

162 The file 'RCaverages.csv' is shown below.

```
RCaverages.csv

Kevin,98.2
Innes,97.3
Alex,97.7
Jackie,92.9
Innes,98.1
Alex,97.3
Greg,98.5
Kevin,96.6
Alex,97.8
Greg,98.5
```

If the user enters "Alex", state the output from the following program.

```
scores = []
name = str(input("Please enter a name"))
with open('RCaverages.csv','r') as allScores:
    for each in allScores.readlines():
        each = each[0:-1]
        temp = each.split(",")
        if temp[0] == name:
            scores.append(temp[1])
print("The scores for",name,"were:")
for loop in range(len(scores)):
    print(scores[loop])
```

163 The file "longJumps.txt" is shown below. State the output from the following program.

```
Summa-7.23-7.34-8.11-8.08
Petra-6.92-7.33-7.92-7.55
Kylie-7.55-7.41-7.99-8.13
```

```
names = []
jump = []
with open('longJumps.txt','r') as longJs:
    for eachPerson in longJs.readlines():
        eachPerson = eachPerson[0:-1]
        temp = eachPerson.split("-")
        names.append(temp[0])
        longest = max(float(temp[1]), float(temp[2]), float(temp[3]), float(temp[4]))
        jump.append(longest)
for loop in range(len(jump)):
    print(names[loop],jump[loop])
```

Output

164 And finally, a very difficult puzzle. Well done if you get this one.
The files "num1.txt" and "num2.txt" are shown below.

num1.txt
10,20,30,40
20,30,40,50
30,40,50,60
40,50,60,70

num2.txt
1,2,3,4
2,3,4,5
3,4,5,6
4,5,6,7

State the output from the following program.

```
temp1List = []
temp2List = []
with open('num1.txt','r') as numbers:
    for eachNum in numbers.readlines():
        eachNum = eachNum[0:-1]
        temp = eachNum.split(",")
        temp1List.append(temp)
with open('num2.txt','r') as numbers:
    for eachNum in numbers.readlines():
        eachNum = eachNum[0:-1]
        temp = eachNum.split(",")
        temp2List.append(temp)
with open('num3.txt','w') as numbersOut:
    for loop in range(0,2):
        numbersOut.write(str(temp1List[loop][0])+"\n")
    for loop in range(2,4):
        numbersOut.write(str(temp2List[loop][3])+"\n")
total = 0
with open('num3.txt','r') as numbers:
    for eachNum in numbers.readlines():
        total = total + int(eachNum[0:-1])
print("Total =",total)
```

Output

Chapter 28 – Programming challenges for Section 7

The syntax covered in Section 7 was:

Statements and syntax	Examples
• with as • open( ) • 'filename.txt' • 'w' • 'r' • 'a' • 'r+' • .readlines( ) • .write( )	• with open('file.txt','r') as conn • data = conn.readlines() • conn.write("My names:") • conn.write(name[0])

Section 6 covered modularity (modular programs). Once you have learned to write using functions and procedures you should include modularity in every program you write. For these file handling challenges, ensure that you write your code with a main program which calls functions and procedures.

As always, the challenges start off nice and easy but will get progressively harder.

Program challenges for file handling

Program 68 – Yearly temperatures

A file called "yearTemperatures.txt" contains 52 rows of average daily temperature readings in the following format: Week number, Day 1, Day 2, Day 3, Day 4, Day 5, Day 6, Day 7.

An example of one row of the file is: – 3,12,13,10,10,8,6,7\n

Write a program that asks the user to enter a range of weeks. The program should calculate the overall average temperature for those days of the year.

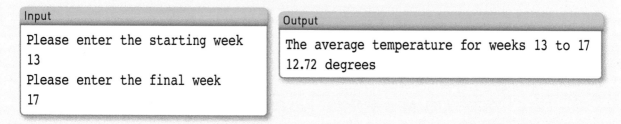

```
Input
Please enter the starting week
13
Please enter the final week
17
```

```
Output
The average temperature for weeks 13 to 17
12.72 degrees
```

Program 69 – Garage sale

When people want to get rid of unwanted items in their house, they sometimes have a garage sale. A program is required to store garage sale items and their prices. The program should have a main program and two procedures:

1 Each time the program starts, users are asked to enter a description of an item for sale and the item's price. Each description and price entered should be added to any previous information stored in a text file. The user should continually be asked to enter more items until the user enters a "trigger" input that stops the program asking for the next item.

2 The program should then display a list of every stored items' description and price.

Input
Please enter description Lego Car (about 20 pieces) Please enter the price 1.50 Please enter description Adult tennis racquet Please enter the price 3.20 Please enter description Bedside cabinet (three drawers) Please enter the price 10.00 Please enter description X

Output
The current stored list of items for sale are: Toy Bear (20cm tall) £1.00 Set of six coffee cups (blue) £2.50 Children's tricycle £5.75 Lego Car (about 20 pieces) £1.50 Adult tennis racquet £3.20 Bedside cabinet (three drawers) £10.00

Program 70 – Displaying chess games

A file contains information about all the moves made in one chess game. The file stores information in the form of standard chess notation:

move number   player one's move   player two's move

Part of the file looks like this:

```
1 e2-e4, e7-e5\n
2 d2-d4, e5xd4\n
3 c2-c3, d4xc34\n
4 Bf1-c4, c3xb2\n
5 Bc1xb2, Qd8-g5\n
6 Ng1-f3, Bf8-b4+\n
```

A program is required to read a chess game from the file called "chessGame.txt" and display the standard chess notation in a more readable way. To do this, some characters in the file should be removed and other characters should be changed to words:

- = to   x = takes   + = check

For example:

5. Bc1xb2, Qd8-g5

would become

Move 5 Bc1 takes b2 Qd8 to g5

Output
Move 1 e2 to e4, e7 to e5 Move 2 d2 to d4, e5 takes d4 Move 3 c2 to c3, d4 takes c34 Move 4 Bf1 to c4, c3 takes b2   *and so on for the remaining moves*

Program 71 – Cinema statistics

A "cinemas.csv" file contains information on cinema screens in the UK. The file includes the following information:

Company   Buildings   Screens   Percentage of total screens

The first row of the file is:

```
Cineworld,99,1008,23.6\n
```

A program is required to read the file data into a 2D list and then display the following information:

- The company that has the most cinema screens in the UK.
- The name of the company that has the highest percentage of total screens.
- The average number of screens each company has at each building.

Program 72 – Yearly temperatures (part 2)

Open Program 68. Edit the program as follows:

- After asking for a range of weeks, the main program should ask for a day of the week.
- A procedure should be written to:
  - store the temperatures for the selected day (for all 52 weeks) in a list
  - calculate the minimum and maximum temperatures in the list
  - display the maximum and minimum temperatures.
- The main program should then ask the user to enter a temperature.
- A function should be written to:
  - calculate the number of times the entered temperature is found in the entire file of data
  - return and display the result in the main program with a suitable message.

Input
Please enter the starting week 13 Please enter the final week 17 Please enter a day of the week 4 Please enter a temperature 6

Output
The average temperature for weeks 13 to 17 12.72 degrees The min and max temperatures in day 4 were -3 and 27 There were 47 occasions that the temperature was 6 degrees.

Section 8 – Standard algorithms

Standard algorithms are solutions to problems which appear regularly in programs. These are implemented as common sections of code. Programmers keep saved copies of coded standard algorithms that can be used in their current program.

Some common standard algorithms are listed below, along with a few variations of some of the more complex ones. It is worth ensuring you have coded copies of these examples.

Running total

A running total uses a loop to add up a set of values. These may be entered by the user or read in from an external file.

Version 1 – Simple example with user input

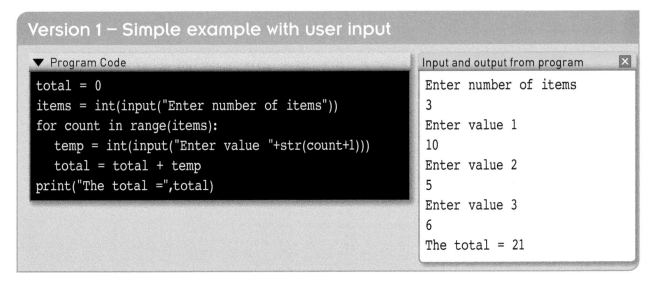

▼ Program Code
```
total = 0
items = int(input("Enter number of items"))
for count in range(items):
    temp = int(input("Enter value "+str(count+1)))
    total = total + temp
print("The total =",total)
```

Input and output from program
```
Enter number of items
3
Enter value 1
10
Enter value 2
5
Enter value 3
6
The total = 21
```

Version 2 – Simple example with data stored in a list

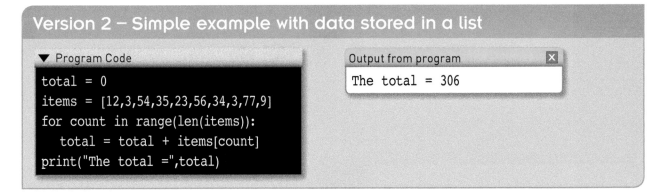

▼ Program Code
```
total = 0
items = [12,3,54,35,23,56,34,3,77,9]
for count in range(len(items)):
    total = total + items[count]
print("The total =",total)
```

Output from program
```
The total = 306
```

Version 3 – Function example where user selects a file to add up

The following example allows the user to type in the name of a file, in this case "numbers". This filename is passed to the function "runningTotal" which reads in the file, adds up the values within it and returns the total to the main program.

▼ Program Code

```
def runningTotal(fileName):
    total = 0
    fileName = fileName + ".txt"
    with open(fileName) as nums:
        for each in nums.readlines():
            each = each[0:-1]
            total = total + int(each)
        return total
fileName=str(input("Which file would you like to add up?"))
total = runningTotal(fileName)
print("The total =",total)
```

Output from program ☒

```
Which file would you like to add up?
numbers
The total = 27044
```

Input validation

Good programming ensures that only valid user inputs are entered into a program. If incorrect data is entered, the user should be informed of their error before being asked to input the data again.

Example – Input validation

▼ Program Code

```
number = int(input("Enter a value between 0 and 10"))
while number < 0 or number > 10:
    print("Your value was not between 0 and 10")
    number = int(input("Enter value again"))
print("Number =",number)
```

Output from program ☒

```
Enter a value between 0 and 10
13
Your value was not between 0 and 10
Enter value again
5
Number = 5
```

Traversing a list

Traversing simply means accessing each element of a list one at a time. This may be to display the data or process the stored data in some way.

Example – Traversing a list

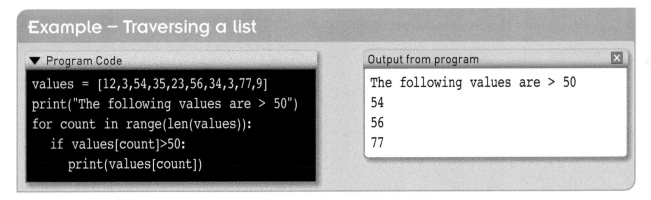

▼ Program Code
```
values = [12,3,54,35,23,56,34,3,77,9]
print("The following values are > 50")
for count in range(len(values)):
    if values[count]>50:
        print(values[count])
```

Output from program
```
The following values are > 50
54
56
77
```

Linear search

A linear search algorithm returns whether or not a value exists in a list, or the position of a value if it is found.

Version 1 – Function returning whether or not an item is found in a list as a Boolean (true/false) value

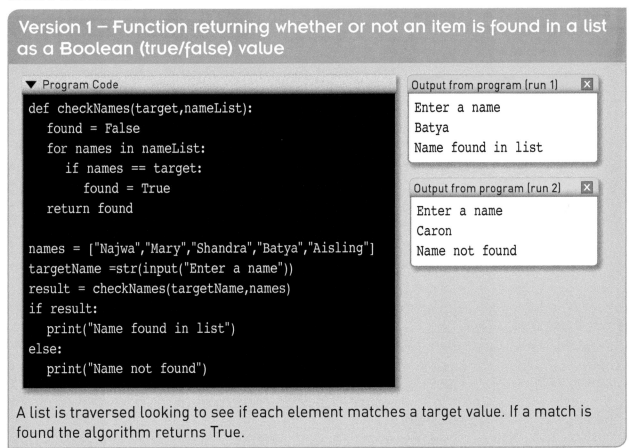

▼ Program Code
```
def checkNames(target,nameList):
    found = False
    for names in nameList:
        if names == target:
            found = True
    return found

names = ["Najwa","Mary","Shandra","Batya","Aisling"]
targetName =str(input("Enter a name"))
result = checkNames(targetName,names)
if result:
    print("Name found in list")
else:
    print("Name not found")
```

Output from program (run 1)
```
Enter a name
Batya
Name found in list
```

Output from program (run 2)
```
Enter a name
Caron
Name not found
```

A list is traversed looking to see if each element matches a target value. If a match is found the algorithm returns True.

Version 2 – Function returning the first position of name after searching in a list

▼ Program Code

```python
def checkNames(target,nameList):
    index = -1
    for names in range(len(nameList)):
        if nameList[names] == target:
            index = names
    return index

names = ["Najwa","Mary","Shandra","Batya","Aisling"]
targetName =str(input("Enter a name"))
position = checkNames(targetName,names)
if position >= 0:
    print(names[position],"found in list")
    print("at position:",position)
else:
    print("Name not found")
```

Output from program (run 1) ☒

```
Enter a name
Mary
Mary found in list
at position: 1
```

Output from program (run 2) ☒

```
Enter a name
Diane
Name not found
```

The above functions could be edited to read data from a file instead.

Count occurrences

A count occurrence algorithm counts the number of times a value appears in a list.

Version 1 – Simple example that returns the number of occurrences in a list

▼ Program Code

```python
numbers = [12,3,5,4,67,7,5,3,5,7,3,2,4,6,5,8,5,3,
    2,4,5,7,8,9,0,9,2,3,6,4,6,2,4,5,7,86,7,4,4]
occurrence = 0
target=int(input("State the value to count"))
for loop in range(len(numbers)):
    if numbers[loop] == target:
        occurrence = occurrence + 1
print(target,"appeared",occurrence,"times")
```

Output from program ☒

```
State the value to count
3
3 appeared 5 times
```

The count occurrence algorithm first sets a temporary variable to 0. Each time a value within the list matches the value that is being counted, 1 is added onto the value stored in the temporary variable. When the entire list has been traversed the temporary variable stores the number of matches found.

Version 2 – Example, using nested loops, that returns the number of occurrences in a 2D list

▼ Program Code

```
numbers = [[12,3,5,4],[67,7,5,3],[5,7,3,2],[4,6,5,8],
[5,3,2,4],[5,7,8,9],[0,9,2,3],[6,4,6,2],[4,5,7,86],[7,4,4,6]]
occurrence = 0
target=int(input("State the value to count"))
for outerLoop in range(len(numbers)):
    for innerLoop in range(len(numbers[outerLoop])):
        if numbers[outerLoop][innerLoop] == target:
            occurrence = occurrence + 1
print(target,"appeared",occurrence,"times")
```

Output from program ☒

```
State the value to count
3
3 appeared 5 times
```

Version 3 – Function example that returns the number of occurrences of a value in a file

▼ Program Code

```
def countOccurrence(fileName,targetNumber):
    occurrence = 0
    fileName = fileName + ".txt"
    with open(fileName) as nums:
        for each in nums.readlines():
            each = each[0:-1]
            if int(each) == targetNumber:
                occurrence = occurrence + 1
    return occurrence

file = "numbers"
target=int(input("State the value to count"))
total = countOccurrence(file,target)
print(target,"appeared",total,"times")
```

Output from program ☒

```
State the value to count
3
3 appeared 9 times
```

Find maximum

Python has a predefined function max( ), which returns the maximum value in a list as shown below:

```python
numbers = [12,3,5,4,67,7,5,3,5,7,3,2,4,6,5,8,86,4,4,9]
print("Maximum value is:",max(numbers))
```

Despite this, the algorithm for finding the maximum value in a list is so common that it's worth learning. Once you know the algorithm you can adapt it in ways that you can't with a predefined function.

Version 1 – Simple example to find the largest value in a list

▼ Program Code

```python
numbers = [12,3,5,4,67,7,5,3,5,7,3,2,4,6,5,8,86,4,4,9]
maximum = numbers[0]
for counter in range(1,len(numbers)):
    if numbers[counter] > maximum:
        maximum = numbers[counter]
print("Maximum value is:",maximum)
```

Output from program

```
Maximum value is: 86
```

The find maximum algorithm uses a temporary variable (in the example above this is "maximum") to store the largest value in the list. This temporary variable is first set to the value stored in index 0.

The list is then traversed from index 1 to the end of the list. Each time a larger value is found the temporary variable is set to that value. When the end of the list is reached the temporary variable will store the largest value in the list.

Version 2 – Function to find and return the largest value in a list

▼ Program Code

```python
def findMaximum(maxlist):
    maximum = maxlist[0]
    for counter in range(1,len(maxlist)):
        if maxlist[counter] > maximum:
            maximum = maxlist[counter]
    return maximum


numbers = [12,3,5,4,67,7,5,3,5,7,1]
print("Maximum value is:",findMaximum(numbers))
```

Output from program

```
Maximum value is: 67
```

Version 3 – Function to find and return the position of the largest value in a list

▼ Program Code

```
def findMaxPosition(maxlist):
    maximum = maxlist[0]
    position = 0
    for counter in range(1,len(maxlist)):
        if maxlist[counter] > maximum:
            maximum = maxlist[counter]
            position = counter
    return position


names = ["Agattha","Elsebe","Ranneigh","Kolka","Magga"]
ages = [22,33,51,49,18]
print("Oldest person is:",names[findMaxPosition(ages)])
```

Output from program   ☒

```
Oldest person is: Ranneigh
```

Find minimum

The find minimum algorithm requires only one simple change to the condition in the "if" statement as highlighted above. By changing the greater than symbol (>) to a less than symbol (<) the smallest value is found instead.

Example – Find minimum

▼ Program Code

```
def findMinPosition(minlist):
    minimum = minlist[0]
    position = 0
    for counter in range(1,len(minlist)):
        if minlist[counter] < minimum:
            minimum = minlist[counter]
            position = counter
    return position


names = ["Agattha","Elsebe","Ranneigh","Kolka","Magga"]
ages = [22,33,51,49,18]
print("Youngest is:",names[findMinPosition (ages)])
```

Output from program   ☒

```
Youngest is: Magga
```

Bubble sort

A bubble sort moves through pairs of elements swapping values where the values are in the wrong order.

Version 1 – Simple function that returns sorted list

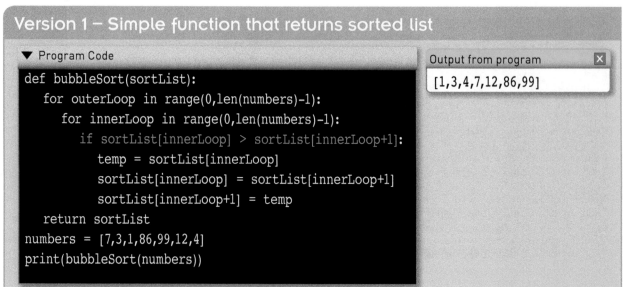

```
def bubbleSort(sortList):
    for outerLoop in range(0,len(numbers)-1):
        for innerLoop in range(0,len(numbers)-1):
            if sortList[innerLoop] > sortList[innerLoop+1]:
                temp = sortList[innerLoop]
                sortList[innerLoop] = sortList[innerLoop+1]
                sortList[innerLoop+1] = temp
    return sortList
numbers = [7,3,1,86,99,12,4]
print(bubbleSort(numbers))
```

Output from program

[1,3,4,7,12,86,99]

The outer and inner loops are used to traverse the list several times. The most important part of this algorithm is the highlighted "if" statement. As the inner loop repeats, the loop variable is used, in the condition of the "if" statement, to compare one element with the one after it.

If the conditions are true (i.e. if the first number is larger than the next), the values in the two elements are swapped.

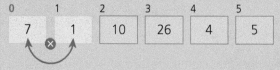

As the loop variable increments (up to the second last element), pairs of elements are checked in turn. If the values are in the wrong order they are swapped; if they are in the correct order they are left where they are.

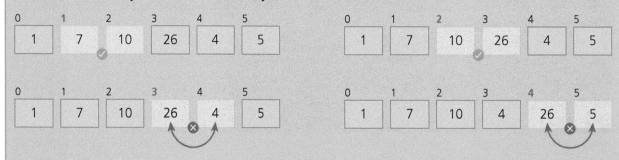

When the list has been traversed once, it is still not sorted. The outer loop ensures that the list is traversed multiple times until all the values are in order.

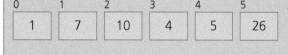

Version 2 – Efficient function that returns a sorted list

Version 1 contains two inefficiencies – these have been corrected below:

1 After the first pass through the list, the largest number will always be correctly positioned at the end of the list and doesn't need to be checked again. Each time the inner loop completes one pass through the elements, it should stop one element earlier. This can be achieved by using the outer loop value in the inner loop range. The higher the value of the outer loop variable, the lower the end of the range becomes on the inner loop.

2 It may be the case that the list is sorted before the outer loop has finished repeating. A Boolean "flag" variable can be used to check if a swap takes place on the inner loop. If no swaps take place (i.e. if sorted still equals True after the list is traversed), the function can return the sorted list early, before the outer loop has finished.

▼ Program Code

```python
def bubbleSort(sortList):
    for outerLoop in range(0,len(numbers)-1):
        sorted = True
        for innerLoop in range(0,len(numbers)-(1+outerLoop)):
            if sortList[innerLoop] > sortList[innerLoop+1]:
                temp = sortList[innerLoop]
                sortList[innerLoop] = sortList[innerLoop+1]
                sortList[innerLoop+1] = temp
                sorted = False
        if sorted == True:
            return sortList
numbers = [7,3,1,86,99,12,4]
print(bubbleSort(numbers))
```

Output from program ☒

[1,3,4,7,12,86,99]

Insertion sort

An insertion sort traverses a list from the second element to the last. Each time the list is traversed, the algorithm determines where the current value should be placed within the previous elements.

▼ Program Code

```python
def insertionSort(values):
    for index in range(1,len(values)):
        currentScore = values[index]
        position = index
        while position>0 and values[position-1]> currentScore:
            values[position]=values[position-1]
            position = position-1
        values[position]=currentScore
    return values
numbers = [7,1,10,26,4,5]
print(insertionSort(numbers))
```

Output from program ☒

[1,4,5,7,10,26]

An insertion sort traverses a list from element index 1 to the end of the list. During this the following algorithm is followed:

1 As the list is traversed, the contents of the next element are temporarily copied into a variable called "currentScore".

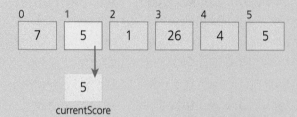

currentScore

2 The temporary value stored in this variable is compared to each element before the original position of the temporary value. This continues, working backwards through the list, until either of the following rules is true:

- the temporary value is greater than the next value
- or the start of the list is reached.

Each value that is found to be larger than the temporary value is copied into the next element.

3 When one of the rules is true – for example, when the start of the list is reached – the temporary value is copied into that element.

Steps 1 to 3 are now repeated for the element at index 2 in the list. In this case both elements at indexes 0 and 1 are larger than the temporary value, so both are copied into the next element.

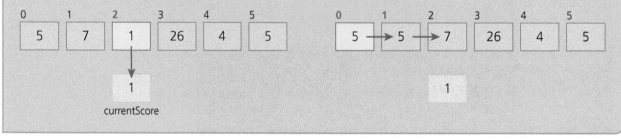

currentScore

Again, the start of the list is reached and the temporary value is copied into element 0.

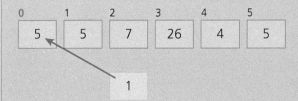

Steps 1 to 3 are now repeated for the third element. As 26 is already greater than the element to the left no change is made to the list.

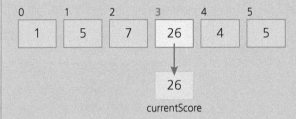

Steps 1 to 3 are now repeated for element 4. This time the temporary value is found to be greater than the element at index 0. This means that the inner loop stops at this point and the temporary value is copied into the element at index 1.

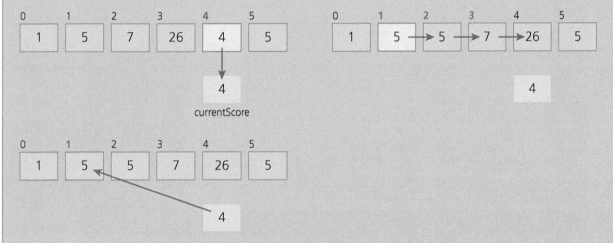

Note that as the list is traversed the values before the current position are always sorted in the correct order.

The list will be completely sorted with one final execution of steps 1 to 3.

Binary search

A binary search works by continually halving a list until its finds (or doesn't find) a target value. the list must already be sorted for a binary search to work.

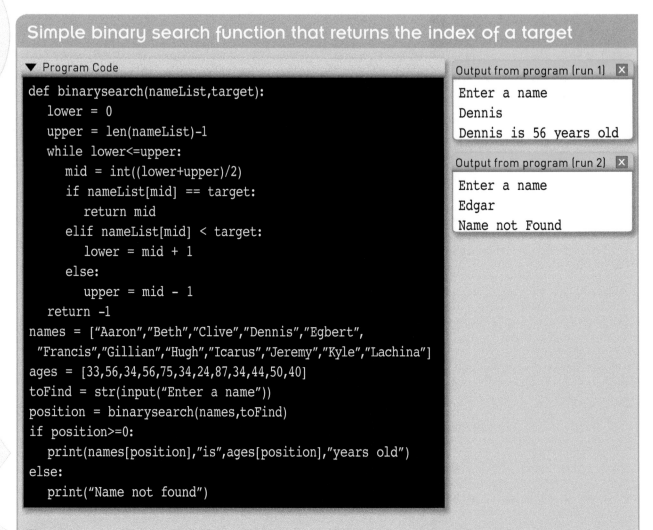

Simple binary search function that returns the index of a target

▼ Program Code

```python
def binarysearch(nameList,target):
    lower = 0
    upper = len(nameList)-1
    while lower<=upper:
        mid = int((lower+upper)/2)
        if nameList[mid] == target:
            return mid
        elif nameList[mid] < target:
            lower = mid + 1
        else:
            upper = mid - 1
    return -1
names = ["Aaron","Beth","Clive","Dennis","Egbert",
 "Francis","Gillian","Hugh","Icarus","Jeremy","Kyle","Lachina"]
ages = [33,56,34,56,75,34,24,87,34,44,50,40]
toFind = str(input("Enter a name"))
position = binarysearch(names,toFind)
if position>=0:
    print(names[position],"is",ages[position],"years old")
else:
    print("Name not found")
```

Output from program (run 1) ☒

```
Enter a name
Dennis
Dennis is 56 years old
```

Output from program (run 2) ☒

```
Enter a name
Edgar
Name not Found
```

The above example has a list of 12 names in alphabetical order. In run 1, the user has entered "Dennis" as the target name to find in the list.

A binary search algorithm uses three values:
- low – the lowest index of the elements still to be checked
- high – the highest index of the elements still to be checked
- mid – the index halfway between the low and high indexes.

When the search begins, the low and high indexes are the first (0) and last (11) elements of the list. The midpoint is calculated as (0+11)/2=5.5. As a list index must be an integer, the int( ) function is used to convert 5.5 to an integer. The midpoint is therefore 5.

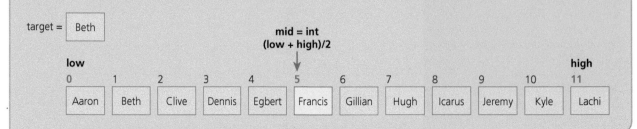

If the name at the midpoint is greater than the target ("Francis" comes after the target "Dennis" alphabetically) then the target must come before the midpoint in the list (between indexes 0 to 4). In this case, high is reset to one less than the midpoint and a new midpoint is calculated.

If the value at the midpoint is less than the target ("Clive" comes before the target "Dennis") then the target must come after the midpoint in the list (between indexes 3 to 4). In this case, low is reset to one more than the midpoint and a new midpoint is calculated.

If the value stored at the mid element is equal to the target, the algorithm returns the index where the target was found (3). This is used to display Dennis' age, stored in the list "ages".

Note that at the beginning of the program position is set to –1. If the target is not found in the list, low + 1 or high –1 will eventually result in low being greater than high. This is the condition that stops the while loop. If the while loop exits without the target being found, –1 is therefore returned as the position. This is used in the main program to display "Name not found".

Section 9 – Large project tasks

For each of the following program specifications, write a fully modular program that will provide a working solution to the problem.

Advice:

1 With larger projects, do not try and code the entire problem at once. Larger projects should be broken down into sub-problems.

2 A programmer should ensure each sub-problem works as expected before tackling the next section of code.

3 Before you start coding, think carefully about the types of variables and lists your program will use to store the required data.

4 Identify any standard algorithms that can be used in your sub-problems.

Project 1 – Speeding

Description of problem

An insurance company is conducting a survey to determine whether drivers of newer cars are more likely to break the speed limit than drivers of older cars. An employee of the insurance company will sit with a tablet beside a speed warning sign. When the warning sign lights up, the employee will record that the car was breaking the speed limit. If the warning sign does not light up, the employee will record that the car was not breaking the speed limit.

The age of the car will also be recorded for all cars. A program is required to store this information and analyse the results.

Functional requirements

(a list of what the program should do)

The required program should:

- Read in previously recorded data from a text file when the program starts. If no previous data exists, the program should create an empty text file.

- Ask the user to continually enter each car's age and speeding data until the user enters 999 for the age. The data for each car should be added onto the previously recorded data.

- Display the percentage of cars that were breaking the speed limit.

- Display a list of car ages showing how many of each age were caught speeding.

- Display the age of car that was caught speeding more times than any other age of car.

- Before the program finishes executing, the up-to-date data should be written back to the text file, overwriting the previous data.

Inputs

The program should receive the following inputs:

- Car data from the file will be inputted with the following format:
  age,speeding,end-of-line

  For example: 10,1/n.
- A car's age in years

  for example, a three-year-old car should be entered as 3.
- A car's speeding result

  for example, 1 = speeding, 0 = not speeding.
- A value to stop the program asking for more car data

  for example, 999.

Outputs

The program should produce the following outputs:

- When displaying the percentage of cars that were breaking the speed limit, the output should be formatted as follows:

  Speeding – 34%
  Not speeding – 66%
- When displaying the list of car ages, showing how many of each age were caught speeding, the following output should be produced:
  Car age (years), number speeding

  1 – 20
  2 – 6
  3 – 0
  4 – 65
  5 – 28
  6 – 12
  7 – 89
  ... and so on.

  Note that every car, from the youngest to the oldest, should be displayed
- When displaying the age of car that was caught speeding the most, the output should be formatted as follows:

  7-year-old cars were the worst speeding offenders.
- When writing the car data back to the text file, the following format should be used:
  age comma speeding end-of-line

  For example, "10,1/n"

Additional challenging task

Write an additional module that works out if new cars speed more than older cars. You will have to consider the following questions:

- At what age should the cut-off point be between old and new cars?
- How will I account for the fact that there may be many more older cars passing than newer cars, or vice-versa?

Project 2 – Election analysis
Description of problem

A national newspaper wishes to run a politics story on the results of the 2017 United Kingdom General Election. The story will include detailed analysis of voting patterns by supporters of the two main (i.e. with the most Members of Parliament) political parties (Conservative and Labour). The analysis of the UK's 650 constituencies (voting areas) will include:

- A list of "safe" constituencies where the Conservative candidate had 15 000 more votes than the Labour candidates.
- A list of "safe" constituencies where the Labour candidate had 15 000 more votes than the Conservative candidates.
- A list of close constituencies where there were fewer than 1000 votes between the Labour and Conservative candidates.
- A count of the number of constituencies (which had any Conservative and Labour votes) where more than 200 voters spoiled their ballot paper, meaning their vote was not valid for any candidate.

The newspaper has obtained a comma-separated.csv file which contains voting information for the 2017 election. A sample of the file is shown below.

Constituency	Country	Total possible voters	Votes	Invalid votes	Conservative	Labour
Aberavon	Wales	49892	33268	57	5901	22662
Aberconwy	Wales	45251	32150	78	14337	13702
York outer	England	75835	57427	146	29356	21067

A program is required to analyse the file and provide the information required for the newspaper article.

Functional requirements

(a list of what the program should do)

The required program should:

- Input data from the file "GE2017.csv" when required.
- Provide a list of safe constituencies for Conservatives and Labour.
- Provide a list of close constituencies sorted by closest first.
- State how many times more than 200 voters spoiled their ballot paper in a constituency.

Inputs

The program should receive the following inputs:

- Voting data from the file will be inputted with the following format:
  Constituency, Country, Total Possible Voters, Votes, Invalid Votes, Conservative, Labour end-of-line

  For example, "Aberavon,Wales,49892,33268,57,5901,22662/n"

Outputs

The program should produce the following outputs:

- A list of safe Conservative constituencies should be displayed as shown below:

  Conservative seats safe from Labour

Arundel and South Down	England
Ashford	England
...	...

- A list of safe Labour constituencies should be displayed as shown below:

  Labour seats safe from Conservatives

Aberavon	Wales
Barking	England
...	...

- A list of close constituencies should be displayed as shown below:

Kensington	20
Dudley North	22
Newcastle-under-Lyme	30
Southampton-Itchen	31

- Note that in some constituencies, 0 votes were registered for Conservative and Labour. These constituencies should not be displayed.

- The number of constituencies with more than 200 invalid votes should be displayed:
  24 constituencies had more than 200 spoiled voting papers.

Additional challenging task

Write an additional procedure that will display a list of constituencies where less than 50% of voters voted for the two main parties. The output should be grouped by country.

Project 3 – Archery scores

Description of problem

Organisers of an archery tournament are looking to ask the world's top archers to compete in their new event. They will invite the archers who achieved the 30 best scores across three continental championships (held in Asia, Europe and the Americas) along with five random archers who scored over 650.

Functional requirements

(a list of what the program should do)

The required program should:

- Merge the names and scores from three tournaments (each with different competitors) into one list sorted by score.
- Identify the top 30 archers from the merged list.
- Randomly select another 5 archers who have
  - scored more than 650
  - are not in the top 30 archers.
- Display the top 30 scorers and five selected archers in alphabetical order of surname.

Inputs

The program should receive the following inputs:

- Data from three files "americas.txt", "asia.txt" and "europe.txt". The file data will be formatted as:

  forename surname score

  For example, Ren Guiying 630

Outputs

The program should produce the following outputs:

- A list of 35 archers, in alphabetical order of surname, who will be invited to compete in the new tournament, displayed as shown below:

  Nikki Bunton 675
  Tandy Cohee 672
  ...

Additional very challenging task

The tournament organisers also wish to include results from the USA open championships. A fourth file of results is supplied and needs to be merged with the other three. Note that this file contains names of competitors that also competed in the continental championships. You should ensure that only an archer's highest score is counted towards the selection process and that no archer is selected twice for the new tournament.